THE PERSON CIRCLE

The Person Circle

*A FIRST BOOK ON GROUP PSYCHOTHERAPY
AND THE SMALL GROUP FIELD*

Sidney Jacob Fields, Ph.D.

Foreword by WILLIAM G. REESE, M.D.
*Professor and Chairman, Department of Psychiatry
College of Medicine, University of Arkansas for Medical Sciences*

An Exposition-University Book

EXPOSITION PRESS   HICKSVILLE, NEW YORK

To Anne Fields
a rose ... my rose ...
not like a hundred thousand other roses ...
unique in all the world.

"A person who's hungry and knows he's hungry isn't going to satisfy his hunger simply by studying a menu and talking about food."

—*Vic J., a cherished patient*

Contents

Foreword

This is a primer on group psychotherapy, with the small group field as counterpoint. It is a primer, with the short i, as an opener for the neophyte. But it is more than that. It is an eye-opener for the mature therapist. It is a prīmer, with the long ī, which will prime the beginner and recharge his elder. And in the sense of vigor, freshness, excellence, it is a prime contribution.

At times I think that the group/group therapy field has become a happy hunting ground for the do-gooder, the huckster, the charlatan, and the self-proclaimed expert, who seem at times to outnumber the ethical, responsible, true professionals. Group therapy avoids the endangered species list, but barely. It survives the predators as a consequence of intrinsic power and continuing development by a dedicated band of clinician/scientists, exemplified by the author, who have methodically moved ahead by constructing, modifying, and testing theory, by inventing and refining techniques, and by establishing quality standards for training and practice.

This book provides a group taxonomy, a guide for further exploration, and a map of the occasional treasures that lie scattered around the landscape. The author adds a treasure by structuralizing and characterizing the unfolding processes of the open-ended therapy group. His chapter on homosexuality is a useful contribution by itself.

The concise exposition is coauthored by Sidney Jacob Fields, Ph.D., academician; Dr. Fields, a professional psychologist and therapist; and Sid Fields, a skilled, unobtrusive catalyst within the therapeutic circle. Years ago Mr. Fields, Ph.D., assigned Dr. Fields to the magic circle, where he accumulated 25 years of experience, day after day, week after week. The good doctor, while helping his patients to help themselves, assimilated and abstracted his rich observations and, as preceptor/teacher, effectively communicated this wisdom to a generation of pre- and postdoctoral students, each progressing from observer, to co-therapist, to therapist. On occasion he donned his academic robes for presentations from the podium. Within the circle Dr. Fields evolved into Sid, a sage and trusted friend, who learned to *hear* the spoken and unspoken word, whatever the accent or idiom, and to *say* in plain English—the language of this book.

This publication is overdue; but now—finally—whether we be client, patient, clinician, student, teacher, or all, we in the outer circle are privileged to participate vicariously in this significant life production from the inner circle "in the round."

William G. Reese, M.D.
Professor and Chairman
Department of Psychiatry
College of Medicine
University of Arkansas for Medical Sciences
Little Rock

Preface

Years ago while taking a course in college physics I tried to learn Einstein's theory of relativity. But no matter how hard I studied the assigned textbook I just couldn't understand Einstein's theory. That I couldn't grasp it was more than frustrating. I was angry with myself because I really wanted to understand the theory. So I stewed for a while. Then unexpectedly I came upon an article on Einstein's theory written by a philosopher, Dr. Morris Raphael Cohen. This article gave me the key to understanding, as it were. I went back to the physics book and found that now I could make sense out of the chapter on relativity. Imagine my relief. It took a philosopher to help me understand physics.

At another time I tried to read James Joyce's *Ulysses*. I didn't get anywhere with it, just couldn't make it out. Again I felt frustrated and bewildered. Then I stumbled on a copy of *Axel's Castle* written by the well-known literary critic Edmund Wilson. It contains a chapter on James Joyce in which Wilson describes Joyce's stream-of-consciousness technique. Ah, that was it! The light dawned, the darkness dispersed. I picked up *Ulysses* again and, sure enough, found I could grasp its meaning as I read along. I finished *Ulysses* with full appreciation, satisfaction, and pleasure.

I have since been ever grateful to Morris Raphael Cohen and Edmund Wilson for opening my eyes. They taught me more than an understanding of Einstein's relativity or of Joyce's *Ulysses*. They taught me how valuable a guide to the unknown and incomprehensible can be. It's priceless.

Such a guide is sorely needed by today's newcomer to group psychotherapy and the small group field. The newcomer of thirty-five years ago was quite able to get along without one. Group therapy and the small group field were young then, and there wasn't much of either. However, the picture has changed in the years since World War II. Group psychotherapy and the small group field have flourished. How they have flourished!

The garden of group therapy and the small group field has grown almost beyond anybody's expectations. It has overrun its original borders to extend in many directions where now its farthest reaches cannot be seen. Varieties of flowers and vegetation which were already well established have been further developed. But wild flowers have also sprung up and weeds are beginning to appear. There are mushrooms in it too, some delectable and edible, some enticing yet poisonous. In this confusion of growing things how does one pick and choose with any degree of confidence in what he's about? Is there any way of classifying the many varieties which strike a person's attention?

The answer is yes.

This book aims to supply a frame of reference that will bring order out of chaos. It is meant to be a guide, a first book, an opener to the field.

A number of books on group psychotherapy and the small group field are already available. Indeed, since World War II the literature on the subject has grown almost as rapidly and extensively as the field itself. Practically all of it, however, is written for the reader who is a professional person, that is, the reader who has received training in one of the traditional mental health disciplines—psychiatry, clinical psychology, or social case work. These publications presume a background of knowledge and a vocabulary not possessed by many of the people entering or preparing to enter the field as mental health workers. For these reasons much of what is already in print must be regarded as advanced reading which does not meet the needs of beginners.

Of course, there are people who do have the traditional mental health backgrounds mentioned above but who are also new to group psychotherapy.

For over twenty years I have been introducing the subject to medical students, residents in psychiatry, clinical psychology interns, and to graduate students in social work and in psychiatric nursing. They all seem to welcome a clear, concise presentation which avoids technical language as far as possible. They especially value brevity. Like the anecdote about the youngster who asked his father a question. His father replied, "Son, why don't you ask your mother?" To which the boy answered, "Gee, Dad, I just don't want to know that much about it!"

In this introduction to group psychotherapy and the small group field I'll try not to give readers more than they care to know. And for those who wish to read on I'll point the way to more.

The decision of how much detail to include in this first book is directly related to the theory of learning which I prefer, the Gestalt theory. The Gestaltists say the way to learn something new is easier as well as more efficiently accomplished when we get an overview of the subject first. After the overview come the details. The big picture comes first, then as many of the details both large and little as we care to put in. It is better to proceed from the general to the particular than the other way round. Other learning theories would have you start with facts and details and expect you to fit them all together for yourself somewhere along the way until you get them to form a meaningful whole. I've long been convinced that that way of learning requires more labor and effort and is therefore the hardest way.

Here I propose to follow the Gestalt approach by presenting a frame of reference which will encompass the whole of group psychotherapy and the small group field. Once you have this framework you will be able to add on as many details as you need or want or come upon in your reading. You will have a place within it to put them all and, like the pieces of a jigsaw puzzle, they will fit together to make an organized and orderly whole.

The reader of a book such as this is entitled to know what the author's position is with respect to theories of personality, psychotherapy, and group function. I would describe my position as a limited eclecticism. Eclectic because it's relatively open to incorporate the best from many sources; limited because it does, nevertheless, recognize boundaries.

Most all of us, regardless of the particular field we happen to be in, seem to find ourselves moving from the known to the unknown. We need to keep ourselves informed and we need to keep abreast of new developments. We don't want to fall behind, nor do we want to allow ourselves to be unduly bound by tradition. We would prefer to be at the frontier, at the growing edge of our field. But here we come to a dilemma, the dilemma of reasoned innovation on one hand versus "anything goes" on the other. Teachers of English language and literature, for example, are familiar with the dilemma, as witness this quote from Porter G. Perrin* in his *Writers Guide and Index to English:* "Because we do not have a series of rules and prohibitions does not mean that 'anything goes' or that there are not fairly definite goals

---

*Porter G. Perrin. *Writer's Guide and Index to English.* U. S. Armed Forces Institute edition. Scott, Foresman and Co., Glenview, Illinois, 1944. Page 37.

toward which we constantly move." That statement might apply equally well to group psychotherapy and the small group field. Indeed, it should.

Is there any kind of guide for the person who stands at the interface between the known and the unknown? Perhaps his only guide at such a point is a quality called "courageous timidity." The standout golfer Robert Tyre (Bobby) Jones* talks about it in a chapter titled "Some Memorable Advice": "J. H. Taylor made the statement that all the great golfers he had known had possessed a quality he chose to call 'courageous timidity.' That happy phrase expresses exactly the qualities a golfer, expert or not, must have in order to get the most from whatever mechanical ability he may have. He must have courage to keep trying in the face of ill luck or disappointment, and timidity to appreciate and appraise the dangers of each stroke, and to curb the desire to take chances beyond reasonable hope of success. There can be no doubt that such a combination in itself embraces and makes possible all the other qualities—determination, concentration, nerve—we acclaim as parts of the ideal golfing temperament for the championship contender as well as the average golfer." So it is with group therapists, T-group leaders, and group facilitators.

What is now traditional was once innovative—the innovative of today becomes the traditional of tomorrow. I was trained in the (then) traditional, which remains a firm foundation for me. I continue to rely on it for the confidence to explore the innovative. Thus what I accept and utilize that is new or novel can be described as reasoned innovation.

Certain men and their ideas have influenced me more than others, of course. First among these, surely in a temporal

---

*Robert Tyre Jones. *Bobby Jones on Golf*. Doubleday & Co., Inc. Garden City, New York, 1966. Page 4.

sense, is Sigmund Freud. I don't accept everything he has said or written—although he kept a tight rein on things, he really didn't want blind or uncritical adherence to his point of view. He provides the foundation in theory and technique on which I stand, as do countless others.

Next to influence me was Harry Stack Sullivan and his school of thought on Interpersonal Relations. The effect of his influence was to free me of some of the rigidities of psychoanalysis. But Sullivan's influence turns out to have been less enduring than that of Carl Rogers. Rogers and his client-centered approach to troubled persons made a strong impression on me. I continue to use it during my early contacts with a new patient when I'm not yet clear about what I'm dealing with in him. It allows me time to become familiar with him and to avoid mistakes while doing so.

After Rogers I began to move closer to the phenomenological, humanistic, existential, and experiential points of view. Which is to say that a person's (patient's) value system, meaning in life, and common bondage to the conditions of human existence have come to be of greater importance for me. Somehow Hugh Mullan represents all these things in my perception even though I am well aware that others, such as Victor Frankl, are associated more specifically with one or another of these viewpoints.

Hugh Mullan is the only one of the persons mentioned whom I know personally. For me he's a kind of bridge from the past to the present, one of a number of impressive people who have influenced me through personal contact. As I think of it that number seems quite long. Some I must acknowledge by name: Jerome Frank, Helen Durkin, Jean Munzer, Milton Berger, Max Rosenbaum, Carl Whitaker stand out—though they may be surprised to hear it. Bob and Mary Goulding and Fritz Perls should be included here. Others are closer to home: David Mendell, Irvin A. Kraft,

Harold R. Winer, Marian Yeager Enete, Rodger Moon, Paul Ledbetter, Alberto C. Serrano, Sterling Bell, John O'Hearne, and Cornelius Beukencamp. They have all taught me something.

There remains one person for whom I have special appreciation. He is William G. Reese, Professor and Chairman of the Department of Psychiatry, University of Arkansas Medical Center, whom I have learned to admire and respect. He has known me for most of my professional life. His rather obvious and self-conscious tolerance of me speaks for itself. Certainly without his understanding and tacit support it would have been practically impossible for me to have written this book.

Beverly P. Wood was kind enough to read the manuscript with a critical eye. I thank her for her help.

THE PERSON CIRCLE

I

Group Psychotherapy
and the Small Group Field:
What Is It?

A typical psychotherapy group consists of from six to eight patients and one or two group psychotherapists who meet together for an hour and a half once a week.

The group almost always seats itself around in a one-row circle. Being seated in the round like this has definite advantages. Since there are no back seats or front seats every person around the circle is physically equal to every other person. Being physically equal encourages the feeling of being psychologically equal as well. Each person is clearly in view of every other person. There is no place to hide, even if one wanted to. In this situation each person has little choice but to be himself to participate in his or her own individual way. Thus (s) he becomes known to every other member of the group and the way is opened for meaningful exchange and interaction.

Being in the round of the therapy group offers you an opportunity to be or not to be, in Shakespeare's famous words. To be a live and living person or not to be—that, indeed, is the question. In the group every member must ask this question of himself.

Psychotherapy groups may be classified as either closed or continuous (open-ended) and either programmatic or non-programmatic.

A closed group is one that starts its first session together, goes on to meet regularly for an indefinite period of weeks or months without taking in any new members, then terminates as a group at a final session. The group dissolves at that point and the patients go their own ways.

The closed group is best fitted for special settings or circumstances. For example, on college campuses groups may be organized and started soon after students arrive for the fall semester. They may continue to meet until the end of the school year the following June when students leave on summer vacation. Under the circumstances the group is, of course, forced to disband. Another good example is the marathon group, an intensive experience where patients and therapist(s) meet almost continuously for two to three days and nights, usually on weekends. All start together and finish together.

The continuous or open-ended group begins like the closed group with the patients meeting each other for the first time at the first session. Unlike the closed group, however, the open-ended group has no predetermined date when it will terminate and cease to exist as a group. Instead, patients will leave the open-ended group one at a time at different times and for a variety of reasons. When a patient leaves the group in this manner he creates a vacancy in the group. The opening is filled immediately by introducing a new patient into the group. Thus the group is restored to its normal size. In this way, too, the group achieves an ongoing existence that may continue for years. It also develops over time an identity and a subculture that is distinctly its own.

Each kind of group, the closed group and the continuous group, has its advantages and disadvantages. It is my guess, however, that open-ended groups far outnumber closed groups in this country. Open-ended groups are found in large numbers in hospitals, clinics, and agencies, and in private practice. Yet with the ever increasing popularity of marathon group experiences the closed group seems to be gaining on the continuous group. Exact figures are not available.

As mentioned, groups may also be described as either programmatic or non-programmatic. A programmatic group begins each session with a set routine, the purpose being to provide a warm-up activity to get the group going. For example, a mental health film may be shown at the outset. These films usually run about twenty minutes, leaving over an hour for group discussion and interaction. The therapist who follows this procedure expects the film to be a springboard for discussion by the members of the group for the remainder of the session. In my experience such hopes were not often realized. The group was apt to talk about matters unrelated to the film, apparently ignoring it. We discovered, however, that even though they didn't talk about the films immediately the patients did in fact gain something from seeing them. They made this clear by occasionally referring to a film they had seen at some previous session. Instead of the patients being unresponsive to the films, as we had first thought, it turned out that their responses were simply delayed. So we continued the practice of showing the movies. Later on these groups asked on their own accord to have the films dispensed with altogether so as to allow more time for direct group interaction. Such requests indicated that the groups had moved into the second stage of development to become genuine therapy work groups, as will be explained later (page 35).

In contrast to the programmatic group the non-programmatic group starts with no set routine, no warm-up exercises. As the patients assemble they greet each other and engage in small talk as they gradually settle down. Then a silence. Tension mounts and with it a sense of anticipation. In a little while, though it may seem like a long time, someone breaks the silence. Something is on his or her mind, and as that person puts it into words the session gets under way. No one knows in advance, not even the therapist, the direction the group will take or the themes it will dwell upon. The freedom to decide for themselves how they as a group will use their time together has deep appeal for many people, though some in the group may not be ready to accept this freedom.

Probably most psychotherapy groups in the United States are open-ended (continuous) rather than closed, and nonprogrammatic rather than programmatic.

Good teachers and good teaching practice emphasize the importance of definitions when introducing new and unfamiliar subjects. Do we have any definitions for group psychotherapy and the small group field? Indeed we do. Many more than we need. The literature abounds with them. Yet all fall short in some respect. The entire field has grown so big and in so many directions it is almost impossible to find a definition to cover everything. This creates a discouraging situation for newcomers to the group scene who eagerly read the available books and articles on the subject expecting to be enlightened, only to come away feeling disappointed and frustrated. They get the impression of chaos and contradiction in the field. And so it may appear. Nevertheless, order, organization, and direction do exist. The aim of this book is to show that they do.

We do not really need a formal definition. We can get along quite well without one if instead we list the necessary elements which must be present to make a group a therapy group. There are four:

1. Patients, individually. This may seem pretty obvious. Two or more, up to the ceiling set for the group, are required.

2. A group psychotherapist. The emphasis is on group; not just any psychotherapist will do. The therapist must be a person with special training in group therapy. Training and experience in individual psychotherapy do not substitute for training and experience in group therapy. Training in individual psychotherapy usually comes first in most teaching programs, providing a foundation for training in group therapy. However, it does not necessarily follow that a clinician who is effective in individual (one-to-one) psychotherapy will therefore be effective as a group therapist. There are psychotherapists who are quite competent in individual therapy who simply cannot tolerate the group experience. Which is all right. Not every therapist has to be a group therapist.

3. Patients, collectively (the group as a whole). The Gestalt school of psychology has shown that the whole can frequently be greater than the sum of its parts. Here is a good example. Seeing the group as a whole makes it possible to observe its functioning as a whole. The activity of the group as a whole is called group process.

You might suppose the above three elements—the patients individually, the patients collectively, and the presence of a group therapist—are all that are needed to be a therapy group. However, one priceless ingredient yet remains. That vital element is

4. Intent. Two or more patients may come together with their group therapist without anyone having any intention at all of engaging in psychotherapy. They may be together for purely social reasons like celebrating a birthday or a holiday, or for recreation, or perhaps be attending a funeral. Only when they meet together with the announced intention of doing psychotherapeutic work does it become group psychotherapy.

So far so good. But now as we take a closer look at this matter of intent we make a surprising discovery. While the group may be in session with no intention of engaging in psychotherapy it may have something equally legitimate and serious in mind: its members may be coming together for self-learning and self-education rather than for treatment. Their purpose might be to learn about and develop skills in interpersonal relations, sensory awareness, self-enhancement, intergroup relations, and so on. And they propose to go about this learning in a special way—by doing, by experiencing rather than by head work alone.

Thus what a group intends to do when it meets identifies it as either a treatment (psychotherapy) group or as an education group. Because the distinction takes on considerable importance you will find it worthwhile to keep in mind. Unless you do you run the risk of becoming hopelessly confused when you begin to do any reading in the field.

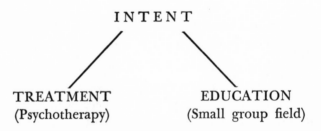

INTENT

TREATMENT   EDUCATION
(Psychotherapy)   (Small group field)

This book bears the subtitle *A First Book on Group Psychotherapy and the Small Group Field* in recognition of the fact that such a division based in intent truly exists. It is a reality on the current scene. Because the public, professional and non-professional alike, has been largely unaware of this distinction it has tended to lump every kind of group together and call it all group therapy. Small wonder the public is mixed up. No one has told them differently.

Note carefully that this is not a question of which is

better, group therapy (treatment) or the small group field (education). The question is which of the two is better for what? Each has its uses and its place in the scheme of things.

Treatment and education are like the two rails on the same railroad track of intent—separate but equal and running side by side.

For the very reason that they do have separate identities our list of the other three elements which with intent define a group needs to be reworded so as to apply to the small group field as well as to group psychotherapy.

Instead of being identified as patients or thought of as patients, persons who enter groups in the small group field for the purpose of self-education are referred to as trainees, laboratory trainees, clients, participants, or whatever. Anything but patients. Because they are not considered to be patients in any sense so far as the group is concerned, the term *patient* is deliberately avoided. Therefore the first element of a group is enlarged to become

1. Patients, individually; or laboratory trainees, clients, participants, as individuals.

Persons who conduct educational groups in the small group field are not psychotherapists, nor do they wish to be taken for psychotherapists. These people prefer to call themselves facilitators, laboratory trainers, change agents, or simply leaders. To reflect this fact the second element of a group is broadened to become

2. Group therapist(s); or laboratory trainers, change agents, facilitators.

Least affected is the third element since in either case it refers to the group as a whole:

3. Patients, collectively (the group); or clients, participants, laboratory trainees, collectively (the group or laboratory).

Try not to let the word *laboratory* throw you. It means group. When you read or hear "laboratory" (or "lab" or "mini-lab") in connection with the small group field simply translate it to "group" in your mind. Otherwise, "laboratory" may leave you at a loss. The term has one clear advantage: a group called a laboratory is not likely to be mistaken for a therapy group.

Putting all this together you see that the four essential elements of any group in group psychotherapy or the small group field are:

1. Patients, as individuals; or trainees, laboratory trainees, clients, participants, as individuals.
2. The group therapist (s) ; or laboratory trainer, change agent, facilitator.
3. Patients, collectively, as a whole (the group) ; or trainees, clients, participants, collectively, as a whole (the group or laboratory) .
4. Intent: treatment oriented or education oriented.

II

Intent:
The Continental Divide

The great majority of groups in this country are either treatment oriented or education oriented. Both are legitimate groups in the sense that they are led by trained personnel who know where they are headed and how to get there.

Unfortunately, the booming popularity of group psychotherapy and the small group field has opened the way for untrained or poorly trained people to take advantage of the situation. These individuals organize groups for their own gain rather than for the welfare and benefit of persons enrolled in their groups. The public finds itself in a quandary in not being able to distinguish the legitimate groups from the wild, irresponsible groups which have sprung up like weeds. Fringe groups are truly cause for concern. However, my purpose at this point is merely to call attention to the fact that they do form a part of the current scene. We cannot afford to ignore them. An informed public may prove to be the only adequate safeguard against them.

Our main interest lies with the large majority of organized groups, those that are legitimate and typical. It is intent that divides all these groups into two categories: group psychotherapy (treatment oriented) or the small group field (education oriented). The differences between the two are basic and far-reaching. A knowledge of these differences is essential to an understanding of the field as a whole.

Group psychotherapy and the small group field developed from two different directions, group psychotherapy from one direction, the small group field from the other direction.

Let's first look at each of the two separately.

Group psychotherapy rests upon the tradition of individual psychotherapy. Individual psychotherapy, in turn, goes back to Sigmund Freud and psychoanalysis. Freud's many contributions to an understanding of human behavior have significantly influenced our Western culture and civilization. The teachings of Freud have touched all of us, whether we are aware of it or not.

Since the beginning of mankind men and women have had to figure out his or her fellow man or woman to know what to expect from the other person. So almost everybody who has ever lived on this earth has found it necessary for his or her own survival and welfare to become something of a psychologist. In this sense psychology is everybody's business. This may come as a surprise to some people. Rather like the story about a man in a small midwestern town who attended a Chatauqua lecture several years back. As he got up to leave when it was over he was heard to mutter to himself in amazement, "Golly, I've been speaking prose all my life and never knew it."

Trouble is, though people prided themselves on being more or less good judges of human nature, their predictions of what the other person (s) might do turned out to be wrong much of the time. Predictions were based on what they knew of the other person and on their own private notions about what makes a man tick. That they were frequently wrong left them feeling disappointed, frustrated, and bewildered. This is the way things were for centuries—until Freud came along. He was as puzzled as others at first. As a physician he was called on to treat people whose behavior was not normal. Yet Freud found he could not treat a patient until he could first understand him. He soon discovered, by way of his interest in hypnosis, that a person's behavior is not explainable by simply watching that individual and using one's own common sense.

Freud found that things happen below the surface in the private world of a person's mind. He found also that these private thoughts, feelings, sensations, urges, dreams, attitudes and past events which are not visible to the outer world have a powerful impact on how we lead our lives, each in our own way.

Freud soon abandoned hypnosis in favor of developing a new technique called psychoanalysis, a method for exploring a man's inner world. With successful exploration came understanding. Understanding in turn provided an opportunity to influence what was going on in the person's mind. This influence, intended to relieve the patient's suffering and to restore him to healthy, effective living, is treatment. We also call it psychoanalysis or psychotherapy, other words for psychological treatment. Freud discovered that certain physical disorders, called psychosomatic, cannot be cured by medicines but can be cured by the opportunity to talk out one's problems, feelings, and conflicts. Hysterical blindness or hysterical paralysis are good examples. On the other hand, there are physical diseases which develop mental symptoms, diseases which respond only to medicines and are not at all responsive to the talking cure called psychotherapy. Advanced syphilis is the classic example. Disorders which are relieved or cured by psychotherapy are called functional disorders. Disorders which can be cured only by medication are called organic disorders.

The principles and techniques of Freudian psychoanalysis are specific and precise. Freud would have his patient lie comfortably on a couch. Then, so as not to be a distraction to the patient, he would seat himself behind the patient's head out of the patient's sight. Next he instructed the patient to follow the fundamental rule of free association. The fundamental rule requires the patient to put into words every thought, feeling, sensation, dream, fantasy, wish, memory or fragments of memories, holding nothing back. Freud was strict in having his patients follow the rule during the entire session while the patient was on the couch.

This free association is, indeed, a pathway to a person's inner private world. Much of what a patient says during these sessions has to do with events which occurred earlier in his life, and his feelings about these events. Exploring one's past life in this manner is part of what is meant by depth psychotherapy. The other part of its meaning is that we move below the surface of conscious awareness to the subconscious and then to the unconscious workings of a person's mind. When you hear or read of depth psychotherapy or depth psychology bear in mind that depth has both meanings.

The psychoanalyst attends to a number of aspects of a patient's behavior. He is interested, of course, in what the patient says and the way he says it. He observes the patient's facial expressions and the messages contained in the patient's body movements, sometimes called body language. The analyst notes how the patient handles anxiety and which of the several defense mechanisms against anxiety the patient is inclined to fall back upon. He looks, too, for evidence of resistance by the patient. Resistance is the psychological defense against the pain and discomfort of bringing unconscious thoughts or impulses into awareness. Resistance is also the withholding of personal information because of fear of rejection, shame, distrust of the therapist, embarrassment, or other reasons.

The psychoanalytic therapist watches also for indications of transference. Transference means that the feelings and attitudes we had toward important persons in our lives when we were young and impressionable are now carried over to other persons in our present lives who in some way remind us of those important people in our past. When this occurs we react to the new people with the same feelings and attitudes we had toward the earlier people. Sometimes we're aware that we're doing this and sometimes not. For example, a patient is almost sure to develop transference feelings toward the therapist because the therapist is likely to remind the patient of the patient's father—or mother—in some manner. The feelings may be positive, pleasant, tender, warm, and loving; or they may be negative, unpleasant, angry, hateful feelings and attitudes; or they may be combinations of both positive and negative feelings.

What the patient does with his sexual impulses and what he does with his aggressive impulses likewise provide material to be explored and analyzed.

As therapy proceeds the psychoanalyst will offer interpretations to the patient which the patient may or may not accept. The purpose of interpretation is to point out connections between feelings, events and behaviors in the patient's life which before had seemed to him to be entirely unconnected. When interpretation is effective and the patient sees the connection being pointed out he is said to have gained insight. Interpretations must be precisely timed. If they are made either too soon or too late they are apt to fall flat and be useless.

Freudian psychoanalysis, just briefly described, was the original model upon which traditional individual psychotherapy is patterned. Individual psychotherapy means variations based on the original psychoanalytic model which still rely heavily on Freud's ideas about psychodynamics (what makes people tick) and psychopathology (what makes people emotionally sick). One such variation is to allow the patient to sit in a chair facing the psychotherapist instead of requiring the patient to lie on a couch. The true psychoanalyst would insist that even this physical rearrangement immediately changes psychoanalysis into something else. We call that something else individual psychotherapy. Psychoanalysis then is only one form of psychotherapy; all psychotherapy is not psychoanalysis.

If it was a controversial change to allow the patient to sit facing the therapist, think how much more controversial it must have been for the therapist to begin to see several patients at the same time in a group. Yet this is exactly what happened. Indeed, by the time of World War II so many psychoanalytically trained professionals were seeing patients in groups that they thought it worthwhile to form an organization of group therapists and in 1945 the American Group Psychotherapy Association was born.

Some of these professionals, who preferred to be called group psychoanalysts, remained as close as they could to all of Freud's theories and techniques of treatment. Other professionals who could not feel comfortable being so closely bound to Freud nevertheless argued that they were still within the psychoanalytic framework as long as they dealt with resistance and transference in their group sessions.

I might point out here that not even all psychoanalysts are Freudian. A number of people who received their basic training with him later modified the theories or the practice of Freudian psychoanalysis in their own ways. Alfred Adler, Carl Jung, Otto Rank, Wilhelm Reich, Karen Horney, Erich Fromm, and Harry Stack Sullivan are a few who built upon the Freudian foundation with their own contributions. So while all Freudians are psychoanalysts, not all psychoanalysts are strictly Freudian.

At any rate, the psychoanalyst who sees patients in groups does attempt to carry over into the group all he has learned about individual psychoanalysis. He is apt to see himself in the group as an authority figure and he observes closely how each patient relates to him in this role, knowing that he could be perceived as good father or bad father, or even as good mother or bad mother, or mixtures of both. He sees the patients in the group relating to each other as though they were brothers and sisters struggling with each other as rivals for the favor and affection of their group father, the psychoanalyst. One or more may also wish to destroy what they feel to be his power over them. He encourages group members to disclose their dreams and fantasies, their loves and hates, their impressions of each other and of him, their physical sensations and, indeed, anything that comes to mind.

The group analyst tends to focus on the individual patient in the group rather than on the group as a group. Hence he either ignores or pays little attention to the impact of the group on the individual. If you watch such a group in progress you are apt to get the distinct impression that the group analyst moves systematically from one person to another around the circle as though he were allotting the same amount of time to each. When he does this the interaction among the members of the group drops to almost zero. They are forced to become bystanders to the exchange between the group analyst and the particular patient he is working with at the moment.

As an aftermath of World War II the Veterans Administration received thousands of former servicemen for treatment. Faced with such a heavy patient load the VA initiated a broad program of group psychotherapy for its psychiatric patients. This action and the knowledge resulting from it further served to establish group psychotherapy as an effective and respected approach to the treatment of emotional disorders.

Now what about the small group field? Where did it come from?

Oddly enough, although the small group field developed outside of psychoanalysis and group psychotherapy it came into being during the same period, the years of World War II. World War II itself had much to do with it, though not all. There were stirrings from three separate sources of activity in the small group field. As time went by these three sources like three small streams ran together to merge into the mainstream now called the small group field.

The first source of information and knowledge during WW II was the military services. Each branch of service on the land, in the sea, and in the air carried out specialized operations involving men in small groups. Tank crews were small groups, bomber crews were small groups, and submarine crews, though larger, were still relatively small groups. It quickly became evident that the success of the missions of these small groups of men depended upon how the men felt about themselves and about each other. The various services began to study the factors making for effective or ineffective leadership; the qualities that lead to cooperative followership; what influences make for high morale; how rumors get started and how they can be stopped; and many other aspects of how small groups function, as in crisis situations. The pressure for all these studies was, of course, survival and victory. Psychologists and social scientists who carried out these investigations circulated their findings through military channels. Most of this new knowledge was classified information and therefore not available to the general public at the time. With the end of the war, however, many of these scientists left the military services, taking their new knowledge with them back into civilian life.

A second source of understanding about small groups during the period of WW II came, surprisingly enough, from industry. The driving force here was the vital need to increase production for the war effort. The push to increase production continued after the war ended, though its purpose now was for higher profit. Industrial psychologists who studied the situation began to see the factory worker as an investment rather than a mere cog in the wheel. Soon owners, operators, and managers of industry accepted in growing numbers the idea that their workers were of first importance and that the human investment was greater than the investment in the physical plant. As workers and their working relations within the plant were studied a marked rise in production did occur. Industrial psychologists discovered that no matter how large a plant or factory might be, workers seemed to work together as small groups, with each group having its own foreman or supervisor. Matters affecting leadership, followership, morale, and attitudes toward management were found to have a direct bearing on productivity. Likewise the relations of foremen and supervisors to the men over them in management or executive positions again took on aspects of small group behavior. Reports of studies in the area of industrial relations were published in professional journals; the literature grew and continues to grow at a rapid pace.

The third source of the small group field is a matter of serendipity, which means that one accidentally finds something different and better than what one is looking for. Since 1936 the workshop (small group) method of teaching and learning had shown much promise. The potential of the workshop approach for changing attitudes and behavior drew the attention of a well-known social psychologist, Kurt Lewin. At the same time Leland P. Bradford of the National Education Association was exploring methods of improving adult education. Two other men, Kenneth D. Benne of Teachers College and Ronald Lippitt of the Research Center for Group Dynamics, were involved in studying the social-psychological processes of building a community out of conflicting orientations. Because the federal government in 1946 was concerned about the effectiveness of the Fair Employment Practices Act these men with their associates were persuaded to conduct a workshop for the purpose of developing more effective community leaders of the FEPC. The workshop was held in the summer of that year. Thirty community leaders from Connecticut were invited to participate. When they arrived they were divided into three ten-member groups. The workshop staff divided itself into a training staff and a research staff. The research staff was to observe each of the ten-member groups in operation with each group's assigned training staff member. The design of the workshop called for the two staffs to meet together in the evenings to review each day's sessions. At these reviews the research staff reported their observations back to the training staff. A few participants asked for and were granted permission to attend these evening feedback meetings. Soon all participants were attending.

It was precisely at this point that serendipity occurred. Although the reason for everybody's presence at the workshop was the operation of the Fair Employment Practices Act and although the FEPC was indeed the subject of the day's discussions in the small groups, nevertheless everyone quickly discovered that they were far more interested in the observer's reports of what each person was doing and how each interacted with each other and with the group as a whole than they were in the FEPC. The observer's comments helped the participants to understand their own behavior and to understand the development of their own small groups. The information about each person's behavior turned out to be more important than the topic they were discussing. This knowledge was a big discovery, quite unexpected. It opened the way for the broad and vigorous expansion of the small group field to become what it is today.

The success of that 1946 workshop stimulated the organization of a second workshop for the following summer. But instead of calling it a workshop it was called a laboratory. The laboratory had the character of a conference, and what went on during these sessions was called training. The purpose for referring to the setting and to the activity as laboratory training was to emphasize that this was to be a method of education and was definitely not psychotherapy or treatment. The idea was to train adults in the skills of interpersonal relations.

Because this approach clearly dealt with adult education it very early obtained the sponsorship of the National Education Association. As the years went by the movement and the organization became known as the National Training Laboratory for Applied Behavioral Science.

That second workshop, held in the summer of 1947 in Bethel, Maine, included what was called a Basic Skills Training Group (BST). Here the emphasis focused on planned or deliberate change in the group and the skills needed by the agent of such change. The Basic Skills Training Group began to be called the T-group for short. It was also sometimes called the Sensitivity Training Group because of its increasing attention to the individual in the group. The leaders of these educational groups preferred to call themselves trainers or change agents. The subsequent spread of the laboratory training model throughout this country and abroad is a story in itself. Certainly the impact of the National Training Laboratories (NTL) has been and continues to be far reaching.

When you observe a typical laboratory training group in session certain aspects of the group behavior are likely to impress you. For one thing, the group rather than the trainer or leader seems to have control over where it wants to go and how it goes about getting there. The participants give attention to the here and now of what is happening in the group; one hears very little of events that have taken place in the lives of participants outside the group. Personally historical material is not deliberately sought out as something for the group to explore: the past is relatively unimportant. What counts is the present and how one person interacts with others in the group to advance or hinder the movement of the group as a whole toward its goal. The group moves as a group to resolve its own problems and to achieve its own ends.

In a psychoanalytically oriented therapy group the focus seems to be on the individual patient (s) while the influence of the group is apt to be played down or ignored completely. By contrast, the laboratory training group keeps its attention on the group itself; the individual in the group is usually given secondary importance.

To point out the difference between these two approaches in actual practice let us look at how each might handle a situation that might easily come up in a group session.

The situation is a familiar one: from the start of the session several patients have been smoking. The air has become heavy with cigarette smoke. People are beginning to cough a little, some notice their eyes smarting or tears forming, and most are uncomfortable to some extent. The issue is smoking, and the underlying theme has to do with rules.

The psychoanalytically oriented group therapist becomes aware of what's happening, then takes the opportunity to observe aloud to the group, "The rule is no smoking." He notices carefully each patient's reactions to his words. One man might burst out with, "What do you mean, I can't smoke!" The group analyst replies calmly, "I didn't say you can't smoke. I said the rule is, no smoking." . . . The man, and the others in the group, stop to ponder what this could mean. At the same time a middle-aged woman who had been smoking quickly grinds out her cigarette, puts her cigarettes back in her purse, and looks down at the floor apologetically. A young woman goes right on smoking, in obvious defiance. Another man in the group turns red is the face but says nothing. Two others stare at the therapist in silence.

As a matter of his own personal preference it may make little difference to the group analyst whether people smoke or do not smoke. However, as a professional working with this group as a trained psychoanalyst he is intensely interested in what each patient says and does when the patient is confronted with rules, convention, and authority—which the therapist now represents, deliberately so. The analyst wants to learn what defenses each patient tends to rely on, wants to know how he/she handles anxiety, wants to understand what his/her attitudes are. By thus taking advantage of a situation that comes about in a completely natural manner he obtains material to be used to further the analytic work of the group.

By comparison, how would a leader or trainer in the educationally oriented small group field be likely to handle a similar situation? He, too, allows the group session to start spontaneously in whatever manner it chooses. He would follow the group interaction as a detached but interested observer, noting the cigarette smoking and how, as it continues, the room begins to get hazy with smoke. He would also notice that although people are beginning to be bothered by it they seem at the same time to be ignoring their growing discomfort. At this point he might remark aloud to the group, "We seem to be having some trouble with smoke in this room." That would be all, no further comment.

A hush falls on the group as each member becomes now fully aware of this aspect of his immediate surroundings and accepts the accuracy of the trainer's observation. A member might break the silence with, "Yeah, you're right. And I've been trying to ignore it. Well, it is getting to be too much, so I suggest we all just stop smoking during these meetings." Another person, who always seems to have a pipe in his mouth which he is constantly lighting, voices an objection: "I like to smoke my pipe and I don't like it when people try to tell me I can't. Like when I'm on an airplane going someplace. They'll let people smoke cigarettes, all right, but they won't let me smoke my pipe. It burns me up." These two opposing points of view move a woman in the group to act as a peacemaker, seeking a compromise: "How would it be if we all agreed to smoke for 15 minutes, then not smoke for the next 15 minutes and alternate that way for the rest of the time?" The T-group leader follows all this with close attention, yet he keeps himself out of the discussion. His purpose from the beginning was to bring to the group's full consciousness a group problem which the group seemed in part not to be aware of and in part seemed to be attempting to avoid. Now the problem and the conflict are out in the open. The group is left to solve its own problem in its own way. How it goes about reaching a settlement becomes a learning experience for each member who participates. The leader of this sensitivity training group is prepared to comment occasionally on how the group is moving toward its goal, which in this instance is finding a solution to the smoking problem. His remarks help the members to learn about themselves and each other as each participant either assists or blocks the group in its efforts to reach a common settlement of the problem it faces together.

This example of a familiar situation that arises frequently in groups shows clearly how differences in intent do indeed influence what takes place in a group. A psychotherapy group, and especially a psychoanalytically oriented therapy group, pays close attention to the individual patients in the group while tending to ignore the behavior of the group as a group. By contrast, a group in the educationally oriented small group field keeps its main attention on the group as a whole; the individual may gain some new knowledge about himself in the group, but this new learning is a by-product of whatever the group itself is doing.

Many other differences stem from this basic difference in intent. We will see what some of these are as we go along.

Students are apt to ask which is best. Well, best in what respect? After exploring the several meanings of the question and offering some answers I usually wind up with a statement of my own point of view. I am convinced that each approach has something to offer the other. Therefore, although I lean toward traditional psychotherapy broadly defined, I do not hesitate to use ideas or techniques from the small group field when I feel these will help the group I am working with. For example, I could be following intently the exchanges between and among the individual patients in a group when it would begin to dawn on me that we really weren't getting any place. Why not? I'd be puzzled. I'd usually find the answer by deliberately shifting my attention away from the individual patients in the group to look at the group as a whole and to note what it as a group was doing and had been doing. The activity of a group as a group is called group process, an idea which comes directly from the small group field. Looking at the group as a whole in this way leads to an understanding of what would otherwise remain a puzzle.

Groups operating within the framework of the small group field can likewise benefit by borrowing ideas from psychotherapy, individual or group. The use of dreams is an example.

This approach, which draws upon the best from both directions without limiting itself to one or the other, I call dynamic group therapy.

III

Stages of Development
of a Therapy Group

As a newcomer to the field of group psychotherapy you may have the expectation that much of what goes on during a session occurs at random. Given the opportunity to observe an actual group in session you may even be convinced you are right. That is, if you observe it alone. But if you watch it in the company of an experienced group therapist he will be able to point out the orderliness which prevails in the group as it moves from the start to the end of the session and in the relatedness of what group members say to each other and in how they say it.

This assumes, of course, that the leader of the group being observed is himself a warm and genuine person who is able to allow the group members to be themselves. Indeed, the group therapist finds he must resist any temptation to take over control of the group. He may be tempted either because of his own natural inclination to do so or because the group itself wants to shake off its freedom and surrender control of itself and its destiny into the hands of "the expert," the therapist. Yet it is precisely by not falling into these early traps that the therapist begins to show his training and competence.

The therapy group is indeed a live and growing thing. Even when it appears motionless something is going on. You need only trained eyes to see what that is. In watching a typical group in its first session and continuing to watch it closely thereafter session after session, week after week, and month after month you would notice that it passes through stages of development. Three to be exact. These are the Beginning Stage, the Middle Stage, and the Parting Stage.

A typical therapy group is a continuous, open-ended group. The closed group is not typical simply because there are fewer of them around the country. I suggest following an open-ended group rather than a closed group because there is a difference between them in the third or Parting Stage, a difference which favors the open-ended group.

The closed group may develop through the Beginning Stage and the Middle Stage in much the same way as the open-ended group. But what happens during the Parting Stage is not the same.

In the closed group everybody parts from each other at the same time. The group dissolves. It is no more. In the open-ended group, by contrast, patients part from the group one at a time over a period of time. This places a special strain on both the patient and the group. But this leaving one at a time is also an advantage because it provides an opportunity for all to experience a wider range of feelings than parting from a closed group is likely to provide. Thus the Parting Stage of an open-ended group has more meaning and more relevance to therapeutic work. Consequently it has more to offer an observer and this is why I recommend it over the closed group.

What about time? Does the Beginning Stage take, say, ten weeks and does the Middle Stage after that take the next twenty weeks, perhaps? No, not at all. Because the group is a living thing it moves at its own pace. Groups even acquire their own group personalities as it were. No two are ever the same. Each group seems to march to its own drummer, each prefers its own tempo. You will see striking examples of extremes in tempos of groups when you observe a therapy group made up of overachievers in a physician's private practice and compare it with a therapy group made up of underachievers found in a Veterans Administration Hospital. One moves rapidly, the other slowly. Hence the stages to be described are not tied to exact time periods. Some groups need more time than others to cover the same ground. Within reason, a group should have all the time it needs to do its work. Although there may be feelings of competition among the patients in a group, group therapy itself is not a race.

What about the movement of a group from stage to stage? After a given period of time (whatever that may be for a given group) does the group just suddenly shake itself and move out of the first stage into the second stage, then stay there? No, it doesn't. The shift is not an all-or-none action where everything either happens or doesn't happen. The movement is more like the sand in an hourglass, pouring slowly from the top chamber down into the bottom chamber, from the first stage into the second stage, as it were. After a while there will be more sand in the bottom than remains in the top, yet the sand keeps on pouring. One might turn the hourglass and see the sand flow back into the chamber it was coming out of, yet with another turn one would see the sand pouring in the right direction once again. The movement of a group is a fluid as the movement of the sand in an hourglass, even moving back and forth like the sand when the hourglass is turned.

The therapist, trainee, or observer who knows about these three stages of development is in an advantageous position because he can look in on a group at any time in its existence and be able to tell within a few minutes what stage it is in.

He would then be able to draw some inferences about the work the group may already have accomplished in the past and guess at some of the work that remains to be done in the future. Remember that every session is influenced by the session (s) which came before it, and each session will influence every session which follows it. The sessions are bound together over time like pearls on a string. Though we can't change this in any way, we can try to grasp its meaning to the fullest.

I   The Beginning Stage

By definition the people who enter psychotherapy groups are among the most anxious people in the world. It is because their anxieties have begun to get out of hand that they feel compelled to seek help and relief from their tension. They come to psychiatric outpatient clinics, community mental health centers, or private practitioners who may be psychiatrists, clinical psychologists, or social caseworkers. Though a portion of these patients will continue to be seen in individual psychotherapy, more and more are being encouraged to enter group psychotherapy as the treatment of choice.

Some may require only a brief interview by way of preparation before joining the group, others may require several individual sessions before being ready to join the group. The matter of preparation will be taken up later (page 103) .

Let us assume that the therapist has seen to it that the necessary arrangements are taken care of and that each patient is ready in his own mind to come to the first session of a new group.

At the agreed upon time and place all show up, four male patients, four female patients, the group therapist and the co-therapist, ten in all. Each patient has previously met only the therapist and co-therapist. Everyone else is a stranger. Not only are all people uneasy on this account to start with; they also face an unknown situation. Who knows what to expect? What goes on in a group? Do I have to talk? Will they like me? Can I trust anybody in the group? Is this a safe place for me to be? How is this going to help me? These and dozens of other questions pop up in the minds of patients as they settle down in their circle of seats for the first time. They are in the Beginning Stage.

Their anxieties begin to show. Perhaps it would be more accurate to say that their individual ways of handling anxiety begin to show. The therapist (s) pay close attention. The patients pay close attention, too, though at this moment they are not as conscious of doing so as are the group leaders. At different levels of awareness each person notes who in the group becomes talkative, who becomes silent, who becomes restless without speaking, who sinks down into his chair as though to drop out of sight, who glares at the therapist, who smiles sweetly and crosses her legs seductively for the co-therapist, who looks dependently for help from any quarter, and so on. The patients may not yet be aware that their ways of handling anxiety are highly individualistic and very much a part of each person's personality. As the first session is followed by other sessions the patients become well acquainted with each other in this special way. Indeed, they become aware of noticing a wider range of small and large details as time goes by. Eventually, when what is happening in the group makes it seem appropriate to do so, patients will confront each other with their observations. This would be early evidence that the group is approaching the Middle Stage of development.

What are patients most likely to talk about during these beginning sessions? Two things. First, their symptoms. "After all," they seem to reason, "since that's why I'm here in the first place somebody in the group must want to hear about them. Besides, how can I expect the therapist (s) to help me if I don't let on what's wrong. Anyway, whatever these symptoms are they are uppermost in my mind much of the time these days and that's another reason they're easiest for me to talk about."

Which quite naturally leads to the second topic the group members will spend most time talking about in the beginning. This topic is a running description of their lives outside the group. The account is apt to be highly factual and quite detailed. At this stage patients seem relieved to give as much information about themselves as the other members of the group can possibly absorb or tolerate. The information, of course, is carefully screened; what each patient allows himself to talk about is the material that's easiest for him to bring out. This means material which he is less sensitive about and less defensive about. Thus it may be some while before really painful and significant events are brought up.

What is going on serves a useful purpose nevertheless. It provides patients, all of whom at this time are relative strangers, with a way of communicating with each other. It also serves as a special and important kind of defense. As long as a person busies himself or herself reporting the facts of his or her life, he/she can avoid saying anything at all about feelings. Later on the group will spend much of its time exploring feelings, attitudes, opinions, and fantasies. That is when the group will engage in its most important therapeutic work. It's not ready for that yet.

The feelings which do begin to come through in the beginning sessions are almost entirely negative. Each person in the group seems to have carefully saved a collection of negative emotions which has gotten larger and larger. Old hurts and grievances, disappointments, jealousies, antagonisms and hostilities, resentments, and on and on in endless variety have been allowed to swell within their beings until it is almost impossible to hold in the feelings any longer and they come spilling out. These negative feelings are expressed more and more freely as patients gradually gain a sense of security in the group.

The sense of security must develop naturally. It cannot be forced. Nor can the group therapist simply declare to the group that here they are safe and expect his words alone to convince them. Safety in the group is something that must be demonstrated, something that each patient must discover for himself. It is something group members start looking for, though usually without saying so, from the moment they enter a group. They look and listen—looking for the unspoken signals and listening for the spoken signals. They are sensitive as to how others, including the therapist and co-therapist, react to whatever is going on. At this point they can be easily and unintentionally threatened by anyone else in the group. So while they are talking about their symptoms and their lives outside the group they are at the same time deliberately testing the group and the group leaders to get some idea about how safe the group really is. In a patient's mind safety and security are apt to mean freedom to be himself.

Normally after a few sessions the members of the group do begin to feel more at ease with each other. The sense of security has begun to grow. Now comes the first real test of whether the group can be trusted. One or another patient decides to take the risk of self-disclosure. He will mention something very private about himself or his feelings that he may not ever before have shared with another person. He does so tentatively, hesitatingly, partly because the words are hard to find and get out and partly because he does not yet know how the others will react to what he says. For therein lies the risk. It is the first genuine step into the experience of psychotherapy. It is an important point in the development of the group because almost everybody is aware of what's happening and of what's at stake. Certainly the patient venturing the self-disclosure will be waiting to discover how the others will receive this new information about himself. Will they make some effort to understand him or will they be embarrassed, try to ignore what they heard, or make him feel ashamed or humiliated? The therapist and co-therapist, too, will be alert to the situation. However, other patients in the group will be equally aware of something special happening. They sense that the reaction of the group to the one making the disclosure is the same reaction they themselves might expect to receive under like circumstances. Those who may never have been in a situation quite like this before feel uncomfortable and unsure of themselves. At this point they are likely to glance toward the therapist and co-therapist for leads as to what to do. If these two people are listening attentively, seriously, with an effort to understand what the patient is saying from his point of view, then the group has the cues it needs and will follow suit. Members will interact with the one who is now the focus of attention in a manner which is non-judgmental and exploratory. The entire episode has thus been a positive one, one which will lead other patients to gather the courage to take the risk of self-disclosure themselves at other times. However, had the group or the therapists reacted to the present self-disclosure in a negative way all present would have concluded that self-disclosure is too threatening and unrewarding to be worth trying. The progress of the group would thus be held back. It would surely remain at a superficial level for a longer period than necessary.

Along about this time, having discovered that the group can be relied on as a place where one can be reasonably safe and where a person can be free to be himself, the group members become aware of a new feeling about the group as a whole. It's a feeling they don't often put into words until much later. It's the feeling that they now find themselves in a kind of family—a kind of ideal family they've always wanted but never had in real life, a family where they can be accepted for what they are, as they are, without criticism or nagging, without pressures to be something different.

The importance of this feeling about the group as an ideal family cannot be overstated. The feeling carries with it a sense of belonging. Indeed the primary goal of the entire Beginning Stage is to convince each patient that this is truly his group, that he occupies a place in it which is his alone, and that he can be himself in this group, "his" group, in a way which is not possible for him any place else. Technically this sense of belonging is called identification. Most of us are familiar with the process of identification in other areas of our lives. We identify with our own sex, with our own home town, with our own school, with our own church, with our own football team or baseball team, and so on. This is one of the ways we get to know who we are. Of course, it also tells us who we are not. Knowing who we are *not* helps to shape us in our own minds just as much as knowing who we are.

Until the sense of identification and of belonging is shared to some extent by all the members of the group the group will remain in the Beginning Stage of development. Once the group members begin to get the feeling of belonging, however, the way is opened for other valuable experiences to come about. For one thing, group members no longer feel like strangers toward each other. They now feel and behave like a team moving together toward common goals. And they discover a tolerance for each other they had no idea they were capable of earlier. They have succeeded in achieving a oneness and cohesiveness without requiring sameness; they have generated a climate of warmth and acceptance without ignoring the presence of hurt and pain. They find they can laugh together as well as suffer together.

The role of the therapist and co-therapist is somewhat different for each of the three stages of development through which a group passes. From what we see the first stage to be like, it is evident that the primary effort of the therapist in the beginning is to ease the way for the patients to gain this all-important sense of belonging. He knows it must come before anything else of a therapeutic nature can follow. Assisting in bringing this about will be his first and foremost objective in the Beginning Stage.

The group will be testing the therapist in many ways during this early period. The trained therapist is keenly aware of this. He knows, for example, that they will try to get him to take the initiative in making the group work, perhaps by persuading him to do most of the talking, even by getting him to ask question after question. He will keep himself out of that trap by simple default, meaning that he'll not oblige them. Instead he will remain silent, though still very much with them as his attitude will plainly show. Another variation of their testing him occurs when they tell the therapist that everyone recognizes him to be the expert in the group. They imply that he therefore has no choice but to offer his advice freely on all matters when asked. Deep within themselves, of course, they don't want to be told by anyone how to run their lives and would inwardly resent anyone in the group, therapist or patient alike, who might try to do so. Yet they persist in testing out the therapist in this way. If he is smart enough not to fall for it, they will respect him. What a patient says he wants and what he really wants can be quite different.

We have looked at the outstanding features of the Beginning Stage of development of a group. In brief review these are:

1. Patients, anxious in their own right, feel even more anxious in the presence of strangers in a situation which is also strange.
2. The characteristic manner in which each patient handles his anxiety emerges as a distinct personality pattern in a short time.
3. Conversation centers upon symptoms or upon outside events in the patients' lives.
4. Patients gradually learn that the group is a safe and secure place to be in, that it can be trusted, and that it will honor confidences.
5. Group members begin to see the group as an ideal family, one they've always wanted but never expected to find, one in which each person can be himself in his own way.
6. Feelings expressed about the significant people in their lives are mostly negative.
7. Patients first dip their toes into the water of psycho-therapy by offering tentative self-disclosures.
8. Identification with the group and a sense of belonging to the group constitute the main goal of the first stage. Until it is achieved the group cannot move on.
9. The role of the therapist and co-therapist is twofold:
    a. To assist each patient in identifying with the group to make it his own;
    b. To be prepared to be tested by the group without falling into the traps it will set, yet doing so in such a way that group members will not feel rejected.

II   The Middle Stage

Several features mark the Middle Stage of development of a therapy group.

As an observer you are apt to notice a difference in the psychological climate of the group which at first you may be puzzled to account for. You would be impressed by an atmosphere of honesty and openness, a general feeling of goodwill, and a lack of malice within the group. This climate stays present even though the patients touch on sensitive topics, even though some are moved to strong emotions, either positive or negative, and even though they may interact quite intensely with each other. You might remark to yourself that the group has really come alive. Silences that used to make the hour and a half seem stretched out, sometimes almost unending, now seem to have dropped out of the sessions. The 90 minutes pass quickly. The group seems a little surprised to realize the session is over when the time comes to leave.

An important shift takes place in the nature of the conversation. Earlier much time was spent talking about people and events outside the group. After the shift reports of outside events drop sharply. Patients find themselves talking to each other just as they are right here, right now, in this place, at this time. For group members begin to see, with the help of the therapist, that what they are like in the immediate present during these sessions mirrors what they are like in the outside world. It dawns on them that they don't have to bring anything in from the outside in order to gain an understanding of themselves and of each other. Increasingly they face each other with their perceptions, feelings, impressions, and speculations. Technically this is called confrontation.

The person who is confronted in this manner finds himself in an unusual situation. Regardless of what his immediate reaction or feelings might be, he knows within himself that the patient or patients confronting him are probably not motivated by ill will toward him but by a desire to be of use to him in his own best interests. He also realizes he cannot pass off lightly whatever it is he's being confronted with. For he knows full well this is not the first time the group has seen him doing whatever it is they're confronting him with—they have seen him doing it again and again from the time he joined the group. So he cannot try to excuse whatever it is he's doing as a kind of accident, something he almost never does and something, therefore, not to be taken seriously because it is really not like him at all. He can't get by with excuses. He finds himself in a position where he cannot deny that that bit of behavior is truly a part of him as he is. He is left no choice but to look at what it is he's doing. Then it is to his own advantage to try to grasp its meaning as part of his makeup, his personality. This is the road to self-understanding. The group supports him in his efforts in every way it can. And in this respect the group can be remarkably creative. One of the most powerful advantages of the group approach lies in constructive confrontation of this sort.

The Middle Stage is also marked by a change in the balance between the negative and the positive feelings being expressed in the group. In the Beginning Stage patients seem to be wrapped up in negative feelings—anger, hurt, disappointment, resentment, jealousy, despondency, hopelessness, sense of failure, and so on. These they dwell upon, and these they express. As the group enters the Middle Stage positive feelings begin to come through.

Somehow the American people as a whole seem to find it easier to express aggressive, hostile, competitive feelings than to show their feelings of tenderness, warmth, intimacy, and affection. This is particularly true of the American male. But these positive feelings do begin to show in the Middle Stage. By the time the group is well along into it these positive feelings are being dealt with about as often as negative feelings. As a result the positive and negative feelings tend to balance out.

I have commented on the remarkable shift in the psychological climate of the group as it moves from the Beginning Stage to the Middle Stage. It seems to me this shift from one stage to the other can occur only when the process of identification characteristic of the Beginning Stage has been experienced to some extent by all members of the group. Then the shift takes place naturally, automatically, almost without the patients in the group being aware of what is going on. What seems to happen is this: out of the individual's identification with and sense of belonging to the group there comes a feeling of responsibility. This sense of responsibility is personal responsibility. Because it is so vital to the further work of the group it deserves to be written in capital letters: RESPONSIBILITY.

The newly found sense of responsibility reflects a significant change in attitude among the members of the group. In the first stage their attitude was one of dependency. They leaned heavily on the therapist—or tried to. When he failed to let them do this, when he provided, instead, an opportunity for them to discover their own resources, their attitudes took a turn. First the group members found they can rely on each other as valued persons as much as they can rely on the therapist. This is not to say they become indifferent to him. They're not. They keep tuned in to him. Only now they've become tuned in to others in the group as well. Then, second, each patient begins to rely more heavily on himself. Thus attitudes change from heavy dependence on others, to interdependence on others, to reliance on one's self.

The group displays its changing attitude away from dependence on the therapist by taking greater responsibility for making the group work toward its own goals. Each patient begins to feel personally responsible for what happens. He wants to see the group succeed. He wants the group to remain whole. He shows concern about patients coming in late for sessions and about those who miss a session. And during sessions he will take some initiative in keeping the group alive by encouraging interaction.

The ways in which group members exhibit their feelings of personal responsibility are many and varied. Their doing it is precisely what gives the Middle Stage a psychological climate so different from the Beginning Stage.

What one person in the group does and what the group as a whole does will influence what the therapist does. Of course, the reverse is also true: what the therapist does will influence what the individual patient in the group does and what the group as a whole does. Consequently, when the group in the Middle Stage assumes more responsibility for its own direction and its own activity the therapist finds himself in a new position. Now that the group doesn't have the same expectations of him as before he can relate to them differently. He does not have to be quite so much on guard against falling into their traps.

For example, a common expectation among patients early in this kind of treatment (psychotherapy) arises from their belief that the therapist has power to heal as though by some magic. From their point of view all they need do is to get him to exercise his power in their behalf. They spend time and effort in the Beginning Stage with this goal in mind. Of course the therapist doesn't have such power. All he can do is to provide the psychological climate in which healing and growth can take place. The patient himself does his own healing and his own growing. No other person can do it for him. During this early phase the therapist has to beware of feeding these false expectations without meaning to.

Patients are disappointed when they realize the therapist is not going to work any magic for them. In their disappointment they turn away from him and toward each other. When they do he finds he doesn't have to guard so carefully against giving them any support for their treasured belief in his power to heal.

When patients no longer have to look up to the therapist on the pedestal on which they themselves have placed him they can look on an even line straight across the circle at him and see him more as the person he really is—not above them but an equal, rather like themselves and just as human. In turn he can be with them on a more realistic basis, sharing himself as a human being. He then becomes simply and honestly, as Dr. Hugh Mullan aptly puts it, the most experienced patient in the group. (Note, however, that he shares himself in their best interests with the focus remaining on them, not on him. He doesn't misuse the group for personal therapy for himself. More on this later, p. 95.)

Many group therapists think of the Middle Stage as the stage in which most of the work in therapy is done, and it is done by the patients. Indeed, they take over the larger part of the responsibility for seeing that the group uses its time to the best advantage of all. The therapist takes a back seat, as it were, as he journeys along with the group members on their explorations into the unknown.

As he goes along with them he will comment occasionally on what he sees or feels is happening. He does this tentatively, as though offering possibilities that the group might consider or take another look at. He deliberately avoids blunt statements that would make him sound like the voice of authority or a know-it-all. He has more opportunity to sit back and observe process. Process means what the group as a whole is doing as it moves from the opening to the end of each session and as it moves from session to session. The therapist's comments regarding group process can often clarify for the group what it has done or is doing. Such observations of process are especially useful when the group finds itself bogged down or momentarily hung up and seemingly getting nowhere.

To sum up, one recognizes the Middle Stage by:

1. A psychological climate in which everyone seems to be working together toward common goals.
2. Major attention being focused on the here and now during the group session, with little or no time being spent on past or outside events.
3. Interaction among the patients in which they confront each other with their impressions, feelings, and speculations for the purpose of promoting understanding.
4. Positive feelings beginning to appear and increasing until at some point they seem to balance the negative feelings which earlier had accounted for most of the group's time.
5. Patients showing a growing sense of responsibility to the group and for the group, thus exerting a greater influence on the activity of the group and the direction it takes.
6. The changing role of the therapist as the group begins to see him/her differently and as their expectations of him/her also change.

III   The Parting Stage

Patients in groups just starting out go through the Beginning and Middle Stages of development together as a group. Along the way a few patients may drop out of the group for one reason or another before they have had a chance to become a part of the group or to have gained anything from being in it. When such an opening occurs a new patient is introduced into the group to fill the vacancy. The newcomer, of course, has no choice but to catch up with the group on his own, however far along the group may have come by this time. But with these exceptions the group remains intact and the shared feeling of being united continues unbroken.

The feeling of being united remains unbroken until the group enters the next and last stage of development, the Parting Stage. The Parting Stage begins on a signal from a certain person in the group. This is the patient who has improved, whose symptoms are reduced or eliminated, whose self-confidence has returned, and who feels so much better that he begins to think of terminating therapy. Of course he will probably think of it for a while before bringing it up in the group. When he does finally mention to the group his thoughts about the possibility of his nearing the end of therapy he provides the signal for the opening of the Parting Stage.

Immediately the group members experience a sense of impending division. Their feeling of being united is threatened. Almost at once, and seemingly in spite of themselves, the group members are in fact divided, not physically, of course, but psychologically. The division lies between the patient preparing to leave and those staying. The situation is inescapable as long as patients ever do reach the end of treatment. They will, of course, as they must. Sooner or later they must go and parting must take place. It is as much a condition of therapy as it is a condition of life.

Obviously, then, the Parting Stage is repeated time after time as one patient after another approaches the end point in therapy. And just as clearly it is the individual patient in the group who brings this stage on. The same patient also determines when this stage closes: it closes with his last session in the group. When he is gone the group goes on about its business without him. Members rarely have need to speak of him again because, if the therapist and the group handle the occasion skillfully, they will have had ample opportunity to work out their feelings about him with him before he departs, leaving little or no unfinished business with him.

The outstanding feature of this Parting Stage is the division of the group between the individual patient on the one hand and the rest of the group on the other. His anticipated departure constitutes a primary concern for all—for himself and for the others. He becomes the focus of attention.

As you observe a group in this stage you will be impressed by the length of time the group devotes to this one patient during the session he is still with them. As well it should, for there are aspects of his coming "commencement" which touch all members of the group. However, the group does not spend 100% of its time on this topic to the exclusion of everything else. It cannot be that single-minded. Yet even though it turns to other concerns and other group members an undercurrent of awareness of the coming separation is always present. That underlying concern can surface again at any time and in any connection with whatever else is going on.

The group faces a special hazard from the moment the patient who feels he may be ready to leave first announces his intention. The hazard lies in the natural inclination of people to avoid the pain of separation, of saying goodbye. To avoid this kind of pain the patient may simply not return to the next session of the group or to any session thereafter. Although this is the easy way for him to go, it is not the healthy way either for himself or for the group. He may not only be unaware of the positive, growth-inducing aspects of leave-taking, he may be totally unable to conceive that there can be any worthwhile features in it at all—other than the obvious one of his own improvement. Hence he robs himself and others in the group of a rich and rewarding experience.

So whether you are the therapist or another group member in such a situation try not to allow the parting patient to leave abruptly. To be a healthy and useful opportunity for all members of the group the Parting Stage should extend over several sessions, perhaps a few weeks or even months. This is so because there are many feelings to be brought out and explored. Time is needed.

Some group therapists try to make sure that the group has the time it needs to do this important work by requiring a new patient, before he enters a group and looks forward to the time when he will be able to leave it, to agree to come to at least three more sessions after bringing up in the group the matter of his leaving.

Although the division of the group between the individual patient who is preparing to leave and the rest of the group is the most distinctive feature of the Parting Stage, there are other features as well.

Keep in mind that the patients I am speaking of now are not dropouts in the usual sense. They are not like the patients who left during the Beginning or Middle Stages who could properly be called dropouts because they left too soon, before benefiting from being in the group. These parting patients are, instead, persons who have become important group members. Commonly they find it hard to leave. Neither the therapist nor the group will have to make any special effort to hold on to them long enough to go through the process of parting. The person who has gained from group therapy and is preparing to leave will want to go through it, as though tapering off little by little. As I've pointed out, the time and attention the group devotes to these patients is one of the clearest features of this stage.

Thus the typical patient who is about to end therapy does not do it suddenly, without warning. He brings up the idea weeks and sometimes months before he actually says goodbye. He has many thoughts and feelings about parting that he wants to consider, and he wants the group to consider them with him. He has come to have high regard for the other persons. He values their thoughts and their honesty. If he has indeed improved enough to be ready to leave they will let him know. He's aware of this and wants their reassurance that he's doing the right thing.

Patients discover there are other reasons why it is not easy to leave the group at this point. They find it's rather like leaving a closely knit family one has been a part of for some time. All sorts of ties have developed. Many emotional experiences have been shared, both positive and negative. There is now a feeling of closeness and intimacy that was not there before when they came into the group. The group starts to realize how far along they have come.

Soldiers who have seen combat together and managed to survive know the special feeling each has for the other. It is a common bond that needs no words. Group members in the Parting Stage feel like veterans in almost the same sense.

The group becomes aware of a mixed bag of feelings. Some feelings come out quickly, such as words of encouragement for the person getting ready to move on—to commence, as it were, much like commencement from high school or college. Also easily expressed are feelings of sadness: after all, we may not ever see this person again. Strongly negative feelings, on the other hand, are not so easily expressed. Yet it is necessary to bring these out into the open as well for they, too, need to be looked at, understood, and accepted. (Therapists speak of this process of exploring unpleasant feelings and attitudes until the patient reaches a satisfactory solution as "working through." You can tell when he has achieved a satisfactory solution because he then shows a sense of relief and a tolerance for those feelings which before had kept him tense, uncomfortable, and on edge.)

An example of a negative feeling that a person finds hard

to acknowledge openly is envy. It is a feeling one or another of the remaining patients may harbor toward the patient who has succeeded in therapy. Anger and hostility, which of course are also negative feelings, may be felt by other members of the group either because they feel the parting member is abandoning them or because they feel they have lost out in a kind of competition with him—he's going first, before me. Interestingly, this negative feeling often gives way to an opposite and positive feeling, a feeling of hope—if he can make it, so can I.

Another outstanding characteristic of the Parting Stage has to do with the patient himself who is preparing for his commencement; it concerns the nature of the feelings he expresses. In the Beginning Stage, you will recall, he dwelt largely on negative feelings about himself and about other people in his life. When he moved into the Middle Stage positive feelings began to make their appearance until eventually the negative feelings and positive feelings seemed about equal. Indeed, this is one of the ways we have of knowing that he was in the Middle Stage. Now as he enters the Parting Stage the negative feelings begin to drop out of the picture and positive feelings take their place. As he gets closer to the final session his positive feelings seem to take over almost completely. True, there may remain some slight doubt, some uncertainty, some sadness, but by and large his negative attitudes have disappeared. Now he speaks of things he would like to do, of constructive ways to use his time, and of the satisfactions he looks forward to in his relations with others. He is cheerful and optimistic.

He also focuses on the present and on the future. The past is still with him, of course, but he no longer lets it take up most of his waking time. The change in him is rather like the story of the dog with fleas. We expect a dog to have some fleas. We also expect a dog to stop what he's doing now and

then to scratch at those fleas. The interruption is brief, however, and after a moment or two he gets back to what he
was doing. This is natural behavior for a healthy dog. Now
suppose the fleas multiply until the dog is spending most of
his time scratching, with little time left to enjoy his usual
activities like roaming, hunting, or just plain sleeping. He
has become miserable and disabled; the fun has gone out of
his life. We can liken the dog's fleas to a patient's symptoms
and hang-ups, particularly the patient's hang-ups stemming
from his past, after they have multiplied to the point where
he, too, is miserable and disabled. When the patient pro-
gresses in group therapy to where he no longer has to spend
his time on past hurts and injustices he can turn his time
and attention to the business of getting on with his life as
it is, here and now, in the present. He is his old self once
again. He can enjoy being alive again.

Clearly his attitudes toward himself and others have
changed. You are not too likely to recognize this change,
however, unless you had the opportunity to observe him in
earlier sessions in the Middle or Beginning Stages. When you
see him for the first time toward the end of the Parting Stage
you might easily take it for granted that he has been like
this all along, that you're seeing his usual self. The same is
true for his attitudes toward others. Without a basis for comparison you really can't tell whether there has been a change
in his attitudes either toward himself or others.

The change, of course, is in the positive direction. He
feels better about himself. He can get on with others better
and take satisfaction in his relations with them. He looks to
the future with reasonable optimism. He knows that his life
has more problems in store for him, but he has a quiet confidence that he can face them and handle them as they come.
He does not expect his life ahead to be free from pain and
hurt; it's just that he can accept this now, supported by the

knowledge that life will probably yield its share of rewards for him as well.

Nevertheless, he seeks confirmation from the group regarding his readiness to end therapy. By now these people know him better than anyone else in the world. Perhaps even better than he knows himself. Do they think he may be fooling himself? Are there things about himself he's not seeing? Is he really ready to make the break? Or does he need to stay longer to work on certain things about himself he has ignored up to now?

Such questions and uncertainties get quick and easy answers in groups operating within the framework of Transactional Analysis. In TA the patient makes a contract with the therapist(s) at the time he starts in a group. The contract is an agreement between patient and therapist that both will work on a specific, well-defined problem or hang-up the patient sees in himself which troubles him. Because the goal is stated so clearly at the outset the therapist and other members of the group, as well as the patient himself, find it relatively easy to agree when the goal is reached. Normally he will leave the group at this point, and indeed, at this point the group expects him to go. However he doesn't have to. He can stay on in the TA group if he decides there is something else he wants to work on and enters into another contract with the therapist to do so.

The role of the therapist changed when the group moved from the Beginning Stage to the Middle Stage. His role changes again in the Parting Stage, especially in groups which are not TA groups. Usually, he finds, the group can handle much of the closing work alone, and he's content to watch them at it. He may notice, however, a reluctance on the part of one or another patient to express any doubts, misgivings, or any negative feelings at all at the prospect of a member preparing to take his leave. The therapist will then encourage the hesitant members to come out with their feelings. The persons holding back at this point are apt to be the ones who are newest in the group.

Occasionally the therapist must take the lead in getting a patient to consider leaving the group. Patients can become so attached to a group that they don't want to break away even though they are ready to in terms of their improvement. As mentioned before, patients begin to see the group as a kind of ideal family, one they've always wanted but never had in real life. It is hard even to think of pulling away from such a family. This is what is meant by patients becoming too dependent on a group.

The therapist needs to be alert to the likelihood that a patient has come to lean too heavily on the group for the patient's own good. When the therapist sees this happening he would do well to bring the matter up in the group so that it can be seen, explored, and understood by all. If the patient still keeps putting off any serious consideration of parting from the group, the therapist might propose a period of time, say two or three months, within which the patient will be expected to leave and allow the patient to choose for himself at what point within that time period he will say goodbye. I have had to resort to this solution on occasion. It works in most cases.

We can summarize the Parting Stage as follows:

1. It begins with the announcement to the group by an individual patient that because he feels so much better he has begun to think of ending therapy, that is, of leaving the group.
2. The patient does not leave suddenly, with little or no advance notice, for two reasons:
   a. He is reluctant to leave persons he has learned to feel close to and whom he has come to depend upon;

    b. Healthy leave-taking covers several sessions.

3. The group's sense of togetherness is threatened by the knowledge it is about to lose one of its members; his leaving becomes a primary concern to which the group devotes much time, talk, and attention.

4. The parting patient explores with the group his readiness to leave.

5. The parting patient's attitudes toward himself and others have changed, with positive feelings now outweighing the negative.

6. The parting patient is realistically optimistic about his present and future. He has dropped the burden of the past and looks forward rather than backward.

Parting is, indeed, such sweet sorrow. It is good to be ready to go. Yet we are saddened to be separated from one or more who have become dear to us.

IV

How Therapy Proceeds

This chapter is written largely for the person who will be the leader or co-leader of a group. However, it will also be of interest to others who wish to learn what the group experience is apt to be like. It will make clear the importance to them of knowing what approach to group therapy or group process the leader uses.

How does a psychotherapist go about his business? From his point of view what is it like to do psychotherapy?

These questions apply to both individual and group psychotherapy. The answers do, too. Basic procedure is the same for either type of therapy.

Psychotherapy proceeds as an ongoing series of

    I. Temporary assumptions, and

    II. Choice points.

You may prefer to use the word *hypotheses* in place of the two words, *temporary assumptions*. That's all right. Hypotheses and temporary assumptions mean the same.

Temporary Assumptions

Since we are talking about psychotherapy, the assumptions we speak of refer to the assumptions one makes about people in general and about what makes them tick, to begin with, and in addition the assumptions one makes about a certain person in particular and what makes him tick. It happens that these assumptions we make in general and in particular are usually not hard and fast and laid down for all time. We do tend to change them as we get better acquainted with people in general and with any one person in particular. So there is reason to call them temporary because they do change.

All of us make these assumptions. All of us, no matter who we are or what we do. The amount of schooling we've had makes no difference in this regard, either. The person who has never been to school makes these assumptions every bit as much as the person who has gone through college. We have to make them for our own survival.

This is why psychology has been called everybody's business. Of necessity everyone does become something of a psychologist. There is no escaping it. Almost from birth we all start trying to figure out what persons close to us and important to us are doing or are likely to do. In a very real way our lives depend on it.

First as infants we try to figure out mother because she's most important and closest to us. As infants we need her and want her and if she's out of sight or gone for long we become terrified that something may have happened to her and she won't be back. Next as infants we try to figure out father—what's he hanging around for? What's he got to give? Or is he out to get me, for some reason or other. Maybe he doesn't like me having mother as much as I do.

Brothers and sisters and other relatives come next and we have to figure out what they are here for. Later on other people come into view in our growing world and we're forced to find out what they mean to us. Are they going to do us good or do us harm? This is vital information, obviously, for a mistake in how we see them or in what we expect of them can hurt us. For the rest of our lives we go on taking stock of other people, and for the same basic reasons: we need to know whether they are friend or foe.

Some individuals feel they are better than others at being a good judge of people. We probably all like to pride ourselves a bit that we're reasonably good at it, though we may not boast of it openly.

Being a good judge of people usually means being able to tell what another person is going to do before he does it. Being a good judge of people in the sense of being able to predict what they are going to do can also be a tip-off as to how well we understand those persons. Understanding and predicting another's behavior are the two things we all try to achieve and improve upon as we come into contact with other people, especially with those persons who are important to us. And if we happen to be psychotherapists or are planning to become psychotherapists the need to understand and to predict someone else's behavior becomes more than a personal need. It becomes a professional need as well.

School learning is apt to make a difference along the way here. One's original ideas about understanding and predicting another person's behavior may be broadened by learning what scientists, philosophers, and novelists who have observed and thought about people have to say about it.

One's views, whether they are strictly original or a combination of original and learned ideas, will largely fall into one or the other of two opposite points of view. One point of view holds that what a man is like or what he is likely to do is thought out, logically, rationally, and consciously, and that he is, therefore, fully aware of what's going on within himself. The other point of view holds, instead, that what a man is like or what a man is likely to do has all been decided in advance, that it is, in other words, already determined. It has been decided either because his past experiences in life have shaped him to be what he is or because supernatural forces have laid down his destiny ahead of time.

According to the first point of view—that behavior is thought out, rational, logical, and conscious—what you see when you look at another person is what you get. It is all there out in the open. There is nothing below the surface, nothing unseen. Therefore it is possible to understand another person, and to tell what he might do, on the basis of common sense alone. And common sense itself is just a matter of being intelligent.

This is also the view which says people are capable of choosing among alternatives on the basis of cold reason alone. In other words, we have a will of our own which we can use as necessary, a will that is beyond the influence of our feelings and emotions. Aren't we all familiar with the caution that we should not let our feelings get in the way of our thinking? Many people have been convinced of the correctness of this notion. Many firmly believe this is the way we should be; that even though it is hard to achieve, it nevertheless remains the ideal to strive for.

The second point of view starts with the first one but finds it lacking. The second viewpoint looks back at the record of trying to figure out people on the basis of what one sees of them on the surface and concludes that the record is not good. There are too many mistakes. Therefore there must be more going on with a person than meets the eye. Things must be happening below the surface, things like feelings, attitudes, needs, drives, and a sense of values. A person himself may be unaware or only partially aware of what these are within him, yet they do make a difference in the kind of person he turns out to be. If we could know what these underlying things are for any person we would really be able to understand him. Being able to better understand him would also make it possible to know what he is likely to do under certain circumstances. This is where Sigmund Freud enters the picture.

Freud led the way in what amounted to a revolution in man's approach to a knowledge of man as he is. The influence of Freud and his followers on Western civilization, meaning

Europe and the Americas, has been great. We have all felt
the impact of these people either directly or indirectly.
Freud, of course, was convinced that one had to go below
the surface if one wants to know what another person is really
like. Freud brought the theory and technique of psychoanalysis into being and, although psychoanalysis has changed
somewhat over the years, it still remains the basic model for
this approach to understanding man.

Perhaps the most popular form of psychoanalysis today
is what is called Transactional Analysis. To call transactional
analysis a form of psychoanalysis may come as a surprise to
many people. Yet it is true that Eric Berne, who fathered
T.A., felt he was simply putting the theory and vocabulary
of psychoanalysis into present-day language and experience.
For example, the ego states of Parent, Adult, and Child in
T.A. terms correspond with Superego, Ego, and Id in psychoanalytic terms. Berne's efforts have proved to be highly successful. T.A. has caught on in this country in a way that
traditional psychoanalysis never did. And T.A. has reached
people who would never have been able to afford psychoanalytic treatment as such. Which is all to the good.

Psychoanalysis is an excellent example of the viewpoint
that man's behavior is determined in advance by earlier
events such as occur in childhood. Psychoanalysis also emphasizes the many things that lie below the level of man's
immediate awareness in the unconscious part of his being.
However, one can leave out the idea of the unconscious completely and still agree that behavior is determined by earlier
experiences. Several important theories of human behavior
do just that. Some that do are the various theories of learning
and theories of conditioning which stem from the classic
work of Pavlov in Russia. More recent developments along
these lines are known as Behaviorist. An outstanding example
is that of B. F. Skinner whose powerful approach and method
for changing behavior is called Behavior Modification. The

past history of the individual has absolutely no place in Behavior Modification.

A word must be said here about religion. Though many people acknowledge some sort of religious belief, many others do not. The religious beliefs of those who do acknowledge it are likely to influence the behavior of those persons to some extent. Many religious denominations in this country are based on the belief that God is in control of everything—of individual man, of mankind, of the world, of the universe. Whatever happens, happens because God wills it so. Religions which see the relation of man and God in this way must therefore be placed in the same category with the other approaches which see man's behavior as determined in advance. Only this time it is not determined by the unconscious part of one's self nor by one's past experience. It is determined, instead, by a force outside of one's self, a force called God.

You may find it striking to note how people have been drawn to the same conclusion regarding man's behavior (that it is determined in advance) for such different reasons.

The following diagram summarizes what has been said:

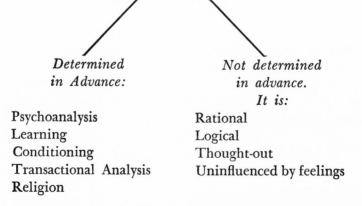

BEHAVIOR IS

Determined
in Advance:

Psychoanalysis
Learning
Conditioning
Transactional Analysis
Religion

Not determined
in advance.
It is:

Rational
Logical
Thought-out
Uninfluenced by feelings

When you enter a group either as a leader or therapist or as a patient you will tend to think of people or of a single person in terms of one or the other of the above general points of view, that is, those either in the left column or those in the right column. You may even find yourself trying to combine the two generally different points of view in some way and find yourself more or less satisfied with what you come up with. Whatever you do, however, whichever viewpoint or combination of viewpoints you adopt will become your way of understanding what is happening in any group session with any given group member and between group members.

Typically these general points of view are starting points as well. Our first contacts in a group, again either as therapist or as patient, will make an impression of some sort on us and we're apt to say to ourselves, "This is the kind of person he (or she) is and this (whatever it is) must be what's happening with him (or her)." Then we wait to see what the other person does and to listen to what he says to discover how close we are to being on target. As the new information comes in, however, we almost always change our first impressions. Sometimes we change them just a little; sometimes we find we are way off and change them quite a bit. And this process goes on and on as long as we're in the group. The effort to get to know another person as fully as possible is endless. It is no different, really, from what goes on in our daily lives outside the group.

How we see and understand another person is important because we're bound to react to him on that basis. We have no choice in the matter because no other basis exists. What we do with him or what we do to him is a direct result of how we see and understand him.

Drs. Hugh Mullan and Max Rosenbaum show how this operates in their groups. They prefer to approach their groups in terms of psychoanalytic theory. Part of this theory involves the concepts of regression and reconstruction. The theory of psychosexual development states first that a person can get hung up in some way early in life. When this happens his development in that regard will stop (become fixated) at that point while all other aspects of his personality may go on maturing. The theory goes on to say that only when a person with such a hang-up is able to look at it closely and experience all the feelings connected with it to the fullest extent will he be able to leave it behind.

Under the proper circumstances, as in psychotherapy, a person is able to go back in memory and recall the event which caused the hang-up and relive all the feelings that went along with it at that earlier time. This going back in memory to relive and to feel again an earlier period in one's life is called regression.

When a person allows himself to regress in this way and rids himself of his hang-up he actually frees himself to catch up with the other aspects of his personality which have gone on ahead with more or less normal growth. For example, he may have found it impossible before to cut himself off from his mother's apron strings although intellectually he may have gone on maturing as shown by the fact that he finished high school and college. As he frees himself from his hang-up with his mother he moves on up the path toward fuller overall maturity.

Because a change in the big hang-up will bring about changes in other feelings and attitudes as well, the process results in the reconstruction of the whole personality to some extent.

Thus Drs. Mullan and Rosenbaum encourage patients in their groups to regress in this fashion so as to achieve, first, immediate relief from their hang-ups and, second, the reconstruction of personality which follows.

These authors point out that there are group leaders who prefer not to take this approach. These other group leaders do exactly the opposite, that is, they strongly discourage their group members from delving into past life experiences. Indeed, they actively assist the members in putting the past out of mind. When this putting out of mind is done deliberately it is called suppression; when the putting out of mind has become automatic it is called repression. Drs. Mullan and Rosenbaum refer to this way of handling groups as repressive. Groups which are repressive contain also large elements of inspiration. Not only do these groups encourage their members to turn away from the past, they will usually try to bolster their efforts by inspiring the members to be better men and women and to lead better lives.

Obviously, the Regressive-Reconstructive approach on the one hand and the Repressive-Inspirational approach on the other stand at opposite poles to each other:

Regressive-Reconstructive . . . . Regressive-Inspirational

I have used the above as an example of how a therapist's assumptions about personality and psychotherapy can and do influence what he does in his groups—the direction in which he is likely to move them and the methods he is apt to use to bring this about. We could find other examples. The point is, know as far as is possible for yourself what these assumptions are at the outset. This will give you a rudder to steer by. Then be prepared to modify your general assumptions regarding a given patient as he furnishes additional data which enables you to make your assumptions more specific to him. Thus the two of you move along together. The experience of psychotherapy leaves off being a fixed, static, unmoving relationship and turns into a live, dynamic, ongoing process.

Choice Points

I have noted earlier that when a group enters the Middle Stage of development the group members assume responsibility for the group to see that it works in their own best interests. Perhaps it would be more accurate to say that they share this responsibility with the therapist—who has had it all along. Even so, the responsibility both feel is not the same for each. There is a difference. Anyone who has had the opportunity to lead or co-lead his own groups and to participate as a patient in other groups becomes immediately aware of the difference.

As a patient in a group you have a sense of freedom which the therapist doesn't have. As a patient in a group you can do and say just about anything you want to, and take advantage of this safe exercise ground to be yourself to the extent you care to be, without having to give too much thought to the consequences. True, you still want to see the group "work" and if it seems to flounder at any time you will be ready to give it a kind of boost in any way you can that will keep the interaction going. Although you feel this responsibility, you are apt to carry it lightly.

But not so when you are the therapist. As leader or co-leader the responsibility doesn't rest lightly with you. For one thing, you've got more at stake, in a way, than a patient has. Well, no, not more at stake. The patient has plenty at stake since his very life is riding on it, on the group, that is. What you have at stake as a therapist is your professional life. You want to be useful to your patients, of course. You want them to be well, to live life to the fullest extent possible for each individual patient. You also want the group to be successful as a group. After all, it is your group. And colleagues will be more or less aware of how you are making out with it. So all told, you are likely to feel your responsibility rather keenly.

For this reason you will, as a therapist, find yourself facing any number of choice points during a therapy session. It is easy to know when you've come to one. You are at a choice point any time you ask yourself, "What do I do now?"

The question is a deliberate one. It calls for reason and logic. Therefore it acts as a restraint on the therapist and prevents him from being entirely free and spontaneous. He has to think out the answer. It may take him only a split second or it may take several minutes, but he does give it deliberate thought.

"What do I do now?" As the therapist searches in his mind for an answer he falls back on all his experience in his personal and professional life, on all the assumptions he has put together for himself as to what makes people tick, and on all his formal training in theory and techniques. He can —and must—choose from among all this that is available to him. And the choice he makes will point the direction in which the group will move.

To show how choice points and temporary assumptions work, let's take a practical example. Suppose you have a therapy group in a Veterans Administration Hospital. The patients are all male veterans, some from World War II. The group is an ongoing group which has been meeting for some time and is now in the Middle Stage of development. A balding, heavyset, middle-aged man who has been silent for the past half-hour staring at the floor now looks up and says to the group, "I feel like talking like a child."

You hear him as do all the other members of the group, who become silent. You ask yourself, "What do I do now?" Everybody seems to be waiting for some clue from you that might let them know how to react. You sense their tension and you can feel your own tension. It's a choice point, no doubt about it.

Quickly you think of the alternatives available to you. Perhaps the clearest of these at the moment is the distinction you have learned between the Regressive-Reconstructive approach and the Repressive-Inspirational approach. If you choose the Regressive-Reconstructive approach you might say to the patient, "Okay. In this group you can be like you feel you want to be. It's all right with us. Talk like a child if that's what you feel like doing. We're with you." Your voice reflects the sincerity you feel as you respond to him.

You may, on the other hand, prefer the Repressive-Inspirational approach for some reason. In this case you might simply pretend you didn't hear him and proceed to ignore him. Or you might say, as though to persuade him, "Oh, come on, act your age! Be a man." He is not likely to voice any of his private thoughts or feelings again after that. Nor is it likely that any of the others present will, either.

The above two examples are possibilities when one has taken a definite position regarding psychotherapy and knows where he stands. This implies that he has received at least some training. But what about the person with little or no training who finds himself leading a group? He might feel comfortable with the people in the group and be smiling and pleasant. However, he might also be leading the group nowhere. As a case in point, take a situation with such a leader. The group is experiencing a long pause, nobody speaks. Finally one person opens his mouth and asks the group at large, "Everybody's so quiet. What's the matter?" And the leader, still smiling, replies casually, "Does something have to be the matter?" The person answers, "Well, no . . . ," and shuts up. Another long pause follows. The group has come to a dead end.

An experienced therapist in the same situation might have remarked, "Yes, everybody does seem pretty quiet. With you, I wonder what's happening with us." This is clearly an invitation to the members of the group to express their feelings about being silent. A member speaks up, then others do, and the group becomes alive again in the interaction.

Perhaps you are now convinced of the importance of knowing what the therapist's approach to understanding human nature is. It is important whether you happen to be a therapist yourself or whether you are a member or prospective member of a group. If you are a therapist, this knowledge will help you get where you want to go with your group. If you are a member or prospective member of a group, this information about the therapist will help you to know what you are in or getting into.

I have heard it said that it makes little difference what a therapist's theoretical position with respect to psychotherapy happens to be because all experienced psychotherapists turn out to be doing the same things. I don't believe that. Experienced therapists do have a few things in common but that's as far as it goes. They seem to be warm, sincere people who are really interested in their patients. And they agree that in psychotherapy the therapist does not take over the patient's responsibility for leading his own life. For example, the therapist will not tell the patient what to do and will not offer him advice. Instead, the therapist will explore with the patient the various alternatives and choices open to the patient and then let the patient make up his own mind among them. Beyond that, therapists differ. A traditional psychoanalytic therapist is not like a Gestalt therapist, a Gestalt therapist is not like a client-centered (Rogerian) therapist, and so on.

Psychotherapy to be effective is anything but a hit-or-miss

procedure. If it's psychotherapy you want, either as treatment or as part of your training in learning how to do it, be sure to get into a group with a therapist who knows what he's doing.

You may, of course, not want or need psychotherapy as such. You may simply want to improve your skills in interpersonal relations or learn something about yourself for your own personal enhancement. In that case find yourself an encounter group or a sensitivity training group (T-group).

Either way, you have a right to know what you are getting into. And, if you ask him, a reputable group therapist, encounter group facilitator, or T-group change agent is obliged to tell you.

V

Advantages of Group Therapy

The group experience has become a striking feature of our society today. It is indeed a social phenomenon. We see and hear of groups all around us. Not just therapy groups, but T-groups and encounter groups and marathon groups and on and on. The group experience is highly popular, highly sought-after, and widespread. It is found at all levels of our society from preschool through college and university, through many churches, and on up through the highest levels of administration in business and industry.

How can we account for all this?

From the bird's-eye view of philosophy and social psychology the value and the appeal of group experience are that it is such a human experience that people flock to it as a retreat from and remedy for the many dehumanizing pressures of the society in which we live. The group experience may make a person feel warm, alive, and human again after the chilling results of striving for survival, earning a living, and competing against others for success. Seen in this way the phenomenon of the group experience is a counterculture which is emerging to offset the prevailing (dehumanizing) culture.

But now let's leave that bird's-eye view and get back to earth. Let's talk in practical terms about the advantages of the group experience. Furthermore, let's talk specifically of the psychotherapy group experience, which is and remains our first interest. I will refer to individual psychotherapy along the way for comparison. However, since I assume you are already somewhat familiar with individual psychotherapy, which I take to be necessary preparation for group psychotherapy, I will omit mention of its advantages. Certainly there are some.

1. GROUP PSYCHOTHERAPY IS AN INCREDIBLY RICH EXPERIENCE. In individual psychotherapy, which is a one-to-one relationship, the range of experience is naturally quite limited. It is obviously confined to two people, the patient and the psychotherapist. In effect it is limited even more than that, for both will focus on the patient. Hence the range of experience available narrows down largely to the life experience of this one person.

The group situation, on the other hand, provides the life, and the living, experience of several persons. One patient can discover firsthand in other persons a wealth of thoughts, concerns, feelings, and attitudes which before now lay beyond his own life experiences. And these are from real people, not characters in a novel. They carry an impact and conviction that fiction can only approach but never fully duplicate. Truth is, indeed, stranger than fiction.

2. MEN LEARN ABOUT WOMEN, AND WOMEN ABOUT MEN. This applies, of course, only to mixed groups, those which include both men and women. Mixed groups of this sort offer broader and richer experiences than groups made up entirely of men or entirely of women.

Mixed groups have a special importance in this respect. At an early age as boys and girls we all start trying to figure out what the other sex is like. And we go on trying to figure it out for the rest of our lives. The question is never fully answered as new information keeps coming in. Marriage makes little difference here. Indeed, it often heightens the need to know about the opposite sex. The mixed group offers men and women, husbands and wives, a special opportunity to catch up on each other's points of view, attitudes, and feelings. Frequently these are real eye-openers. Where else can one get this kind of understanding?

3. DISCOVERY: "NOT ALONE IN THE BOAT." Yes, in the group patients discover they are not alone in their anxieties and worries, their headaches and their heartaches. True, in individual therapy the therapist might assure the patient that he has seen other patients with the same symptoms or assure him that the patient's condition is one which is well known. If the patient then accepts the assurance at all it is because he has faith in the therapist. And this kind of faith is apt to be pretty shaky. Certainly it doesn't carry the conviction that comes with discovering something firsthand for oneself with one's own eyes and ears. In the group patients learn for themselves they are not alone.

There is more to this than is immediately apparent. To realize its full importance we must be aware of the way emotional troubles and symptoms usually develop. They develop in silence and, in a manner of speaking, in the dark; for the person whose anxieties begin to grow and get almost out of hand and whose anxieties may turn into symptoms of various sorts often sees all this as a sign of weakness in himself (or herself) . Since he sees it as a weakness he is ashamed of it. Being ashamed of it he is not likely to talk about it with others. So in the silence it continues to grow.

Now contrast this situation with the onset of a physical ailment. Suppose a person develops a pain in the abdomen. Instead of going away, it gets worse. When it gets bad enough he goes to see his physician. The doctor tells him he's got appendicitis and the appendix has to come out. The patient goes home, discusses his illness with his family, informs his boss so as to obtain sick leave from his job, and enters the hospital for the operation. All this time the patient is quite open about his trouble. He is ready and willing to talk with anyone about it. He knows that countless others have had appendicitis and that most of them have undergone surgery to remove the inflamed appendix. He knows, too, that most of the people who have had an appendectomy have made easy recoveries. So in the great majority of cases the patient is well prepared for his operation. Indeed, when it's over he'll talk about it with one and all—and if you show any curiosity he will eagerly and proudly let you see his scar. Chances are he will engage in many lively conversations with others who are just as ready to tell about their operations and hospital experiences.

But the person with emotional troubles doesn't have the benefit of all this openness. Usually not until he enters a therapy group does he find a convincing answer to that nagging question in the back of his mind: "Is there anyone else like me?" Now he knows there is, and his relief is there for all to see. The first burden (of silence and doubt) is lifted.

4. NEWCOMERS LEARN FROM MEMBERS ALREADY IN THE GROUP. I was about to say, "Newcomers learn from older group members." Then I realized "older" could be taken to mean older in age than the newcomer. This happens to be true, just as it happens that in the group people older in years can and do learn from people younger in years. But I intended "older" in the sense of members who have been in the group longer, regardless of their actual ages.

In individual psychotherapy the patient is alone with the therapist. If the patient has never been in individual therapy before he is not quite sure what to expect or how to use the time allotted to him. The therapist might try to ease him along, of course. Nevertheless, the patient is largely on his own. At times the pressure and the load of carrying through till the end of the hour seem almost too heavy to bear. This may be due, in part at least, to resistance in the psycho-analytic sense. It may also be due, again in part, to the fact that the patient has been given no instructions as to how to proceed unless he is in classical psychoanalysis and is follow-ing the fundamental rule of free association.

In group therapy, on the other hand, the newcomer can sit and observe how the group members who are already fa-miliar with the experience of being in a group actually use the group time. He becomes acquainted with the values within the group. For example, he notes that the person who is open is admired more highly than the person who is closed and secretive; that the person who expresses feelings is ad-mired more highly than the person who prides himself on sticking to the facts; that the person who focuses on what is going on between and among the patients present during a session is more highly admired than the person who can only talk about things that are happening to him on the outside away from the group; that the person who relates his dreams to the group is more highly admired than the person who can never seem to remember his dreams; and so on. While the newcomer is taking all this in he is under no pressure to talk, although he is welcome to join in at any time. He watches with intense interest as an experienced group mem-ber takes the risk of a self-disclosure or the risk of confronting another member with his feelings about that member, and the newcomer is much aware of the reaction of the other group members to these events.

This kind of learning by direct observation is far more meaningful and powerful and requires less effort than the kind of learning where one is told what to do.

5. GROUP MEMBERS RECOGNIZE THE PROG-RESS THEY HAVE MADE WHEN NEWCOMERS EN-TER THE GROUP. In a sense this is the opposite side of the coin from the advantage described above. Not only does the newcomer benefit in a special way when he first enters

an ongoing therapy group. Patients already in the group also gain from his entry at the time he comes in.

To appreciate this point you must understand the nature of successful psychotherapy for the individual patient. It involves changes in feelings, attitudes, and perceptions. Usually these changes occur gradually, slowly, a little bit at a time. There are exceptions, of course. Popular versions of psychotherapy which appear on television and in the movies would have us believe that successful therapy is highly dramatic. A troubled person's closely guarded secret is recovered from his unconscious and lo! he is well and happy again. Such dramatic recoveries do occur once in a while in real life psychotherapy, but they are the exceptions, not the rule. Even the more dramatic of the established procedures in psychotherapy, such as the Gestalt approach or hypnotherapy, work on small changes at a time.

Because these shifts in feelings, attitudes, and perceptions do come about so gradually and unobtrusively people in therapy are frequently unaware that it is happening to them. Or if they are somewhat aware of it they may still not be aware of the degree of the change that has taken place.

Unaware, that is, until a new patient joins the group. Then, as the newcomer describes the anxieties and troubled feelings that make him seek treatment, it often suddenly strikes them and they think, "Gee, I used to feel that way but I don't any more. I just didn't realize it until he (or she) started talking." This is a good example of what the Gestalt school of psychology calls the Aha! experience, a sudden flash of intellectual and/or emotional understanding.

Quite obviously, opportunities like this do not exist in individual psychotherapy. The patient has to find other ways to assess his progress.

6. COMMUNICATION BARRIERS DUE TO DIFFERENCES IN EDUCATION ARE OVERCOME. At first

glance this may seem self-evident. However, the idea war-
rants closer examination because there are angles to it we
seldom think about.

To begin with, those of us who have gotten through college and graduate or professional school often fail to realize
how far removed we are from the person who got no farther
than graduation from high school. Of course, we are even
farther removed from the person who got no farther than
elementary school.

Perhaps that sounds rather undemocratic and makes us
feel uncomfortable. Aren't we led to believe all people should
be equal, even when we know they are not? This vague sense
of guilt may be one reason why we tend to make little of
such differences or to ignore them completely. After all, we
tell ourselves, we do speak the same language, don't we?

Well, take a look at it. Do we? Sure, we all speak English.
That makes it possible for us to get around in most places
in this country and in the other English-speaking countries.
But how much of the language of the ghetto, of the inner
city, do we understand? Or how well do we make out the
words to the rock and soul music which is so much a part of
the current scene? That's English too. Apparently people
can speak English without talking the same language.

Perhaps these are extremes. Although we are able to recognize them when they are pointed out, most of us are inclined to put them out of mind as we go about our daily
business. Generally we are able to communicate with those
we need to within the arena in which we live our lives.

The communication between therapist and patient often
constitutes an exception to this general rule of being able
to get across to those we need to.

The exception does not include the communications between patient and therapist in psychoanalytically oriented

psychotherapy. People who go into psychoanalytically oriented therapy tend to be well-educated persons whose educational level is close to that of the therapist. Indeed, it is
sometimes higher than his.

However, for the person in types of psychotherapy other
than psychoanalysis, and this takes in a greater number of
people by far, the differences in education may be a cause
of difficulty for both parties.

To begin with, and most obviously, the therapist is apt
to use words which are unfamiliar to the patient even though
he may not intend to do so. He has learned to express himself this way and the words come naturally, almost without
his being aware of them. Even when he deliberately avoids
technical words or the jargon of psychotherapy he may still
use the bigger words in the dictionary. And the patient can
be baffled as easily by the big words as by the technical words.

The words themselves, however, only form a kind of front
behind which lie more subtle differences between patient
and therapist. The therapist's choice of words, regardless of
whether they are technical words or just the bigger dictionary
words, reflect special knowledge, special concepts, and special
ways of thinking—special meaning limited to persons with
higher education than average. These words stand as short-
hand expressions for complicated ideas and information the
patient does not possess. He strives to understand them, of
course, as he hears them. Usually this means guessing and his
guesses can be quite wild and wide of the mark. When he's
forced to guess he feels uncomfortable, out of touch, and
put down. He finds it hard to follow the therapist and begins
to sense that the therapist doesn't really understand him or
see things from his, the patient's, point of view. He feels at
a loss, yet there is nothing much he can do about it.

Let's look at the difference education makes in another

way. When people who have gotten as far as senior high school or farther want information on some topic they will as a rule find a book on the subject and read up on it. If we want to know something about biology, for example, we will go to a textbook on biology; if we want to know something about government, we'll go to a civics book; if we want to know something about human behavior and human relations, we'll go to a book on psychology. And so on. The whole world is available to us through books. Books are resources to count on in our efforts to understand the world we live in.

Now consider the situation of the man, or woman, who has gone to school long enough to have barely learned to read. Not long enough, surely, to have really discovered the world of books. He finds his reading narrowed down to very little. He may hardly ever read a newspaper or perhaps glance at it only briefly when he does. This happens to describe a vast number of people in our society.

These same people, it turns out, are frequent readers of the best selling book of all time—the Bible. It may be the only book they ever read or make an effort to read. The Bible is important to them and they seem bound to it, depending on it not only for guidance in life but also as a source of information. The Bible is where they go to find answers to all questions, no matter what.* The large number of readers like this may help to explain why the Bible does stay on the best seller list.

Try to imagine what it might be like to be in the same boat. Suppose you had only one book to go to for an answer to all things. When you do this you begin to get some idea of what it must be like for such people. When I try this I

---

*Here I am not discussing the Bible as a source of inspiration, strength, and comfort—as it is to many people regardless of educational level.

get the feeling of being cramped; of being very small in a very large world; of being on the fringe of events going on about me and of being unable to grasp the significance of those events or of their connections with other events even though I'm vaguely aware there must be some; of being frustrated, blocked, and angry; and of being forced to rely on faith rather than knowledge. I realize, of course, that my feelings only approximate what these persons must actually feel. Yet the exercise does help me to appreciate something of the differences that exist.

There is another element which seems to mark the middle level of education, roughly including junior high school and senior high school. If you think back you may remember it in your own experience. It is a subtle one, although its psychological consequence is not subtle at all: the firm, underlying belief that if a thing appears in print it must be true.

Almost everyone I've ever talked with about this has acknowledged passing through a stage in his life when this was true. Countless numbers of grown-ups must still believe it to be true, that if they read something in the newspaper or magazine it must be so.

Interestingly, this belief doesn't stop with reading matter. Nowadays it extends to movies and television as well. I know one grown woman who is convinced of the existence of vampires and werewolves simply because she has seen them in the movies and on TV. She won't accept that they are make-believe even if they are in the movies.

This example may seem to be an extreme. It is, in a sense. Yet even the most sophisticated among us need to be on guard against believing some of what we see in the movies or on TV. Separating fact from fiction is not always easy. As a case in point, take certain life styles and living conditions as Hollywood shows them to us. Too often we're apt to accept them uncritically as accurate portrayals of how rich people or poor people or city people or country people really live, especially when we have little or no firsthand experience with that particular way of life for ourselves.

No matter how much education we happen to have there is always more to learn. Its just that some people have more to learn than others. And sometimes people need to unlearn. Like using big words when shorter ones will do. Often a person who uses big words is hiding behind them. In groups —therapy groups, T-groups, or encounter groups alike—he soon finds that it is better to drop the big words. President Franklin Roosevelt beautifully demonstrated in his fireside chats to the nation during the later years of the Depression and until his death in World War II how to express even complicated ideas in simple language almost everyone could understand. People in all walks of life felt he was talking their language and therefore talking directly to them. For that reason they felt closer to him. The nation was drawn together around him. It is doubtful he could have achieved this result had he used words that went over most people's heads.

President Roosevelt was able to talk to people in this manner without talking down or being patronizing. We can do likewise. The key seems to lie in one's attitude. When our attitude is one of a sincere desire to be understood, as well as to understand, we find we use clear, simple language easily and naturally without pretense and without phoniness.

I know from personal experience what is meant by having to unlearn something about spoken and written English. In my years as a graduate student working toward my doctoral degree I learned to be more and more precise in my thinking and consequently in the language I had to use to convey my thoughts. Getting that Ph.D. was of utmost importance, so I

did what I had to do to get it. I succeeded. But I found that
in the process I had almost forgotten how to speak plain
English. So I've had to unlearn that part of my training in
graduate school and have spent the years since then learning
to speak plain English all over again.

Groups are fascinating when they are allowed to be spontaneous, when they feel free to be themselves. They are especially fascinating when group members become so intent
on expressing themselves that they use words which aren't
even in the dictionary. These may be made-up words or just
sounds. The surprising thing, however, is that nobody in
the group ever seems to need an explanation or definition.
The new word is immediately understood. An example
which comes to mind is "flusterated." You won't find it in
the dictionary. Flusterated appears to be a combination of
flustered and frustrated and describes exactly the feelings of
the person who used it. This, too, is the English language—
as it is, not as purists would have it.

In small groups people do learn how to communicate
with each other directly, regardless of differences in education.

7. GROUP INTERACTION AND DISCUSSION
SERVES TO STIMULATE MEMORIES, FEELINGS,
AND ATTITUDES.

In individual therapy the patient is pretty much on his
own. The extreme example, of course, is found in classical
psychoanalysis where he is required to follow the fundamental rule of free association. To do this he lies on a couch with
the analyst seated behind him out of sight. Talkative persons
are able to do this fairly easily. Others find it difficult. The
analyst remains silent much of the time.

Even in modern forms of individual psychotherapy where
patient and therapist sit facing each other and the therapist

is not silent the burden still falls on the patient. The extreme example, opposite from the one before, is where the patient becomes the target of endless questions put to him by the therapist. Many patients simply freeze under these circumstances. They answer briefly or not at all. The end of the interview seems never to come quickly enough and they are glad to escape when it is over. Such sessions may be useful (to the therapist) for diagnostic purposes but they accomplish little in the way of psychotherapy.

By contrast the person in a group experiences many different kinds of stimuli. These stimuli may touch him in any number of ways, prompting him to respond. They reach him even when he is silent, passively observing what is going on around him. Yet the freedom to be silent, of not being under pressure to talk if he so chooses, is in itself an advantage. It affords a feeling of safety and relief which in turn leads to a readiness to enter into the group's discussion.

The topic under discussion and the ideas being expressed in the group call up thoughts and memories in the listener. And these thoughts and memories may at the same time be loaded with feelings, some of which are positive, some negative, some strong, some weak.

The spoken verbal exchanges among group members are by no means the only stimuli to which persons respond. Words are not always necessary. Sometimes they even get in the way. Gestures and facial expressions don't need words. They come across and we react to them. We take notice not only of what others are saying but also of what they are doing. A tightly clenched fist, a look of boredom, a worried expression, a foot constantly tapping will attract attention. So will a number of other actions without words. A person noticing these wordless actions cannot help wondering what they might mean, what might have caused them. He might even become aware of doing the same thing himself. Often he becomes so stirred he will say something about it out loud. At that moment he is no longer a passive member of the group: he is active and involved.

The word exchange provides one source of stimuli in a group. Non-verbal behavior provides a second source of stimuli. There is yet a third source, a subtle and powerful one. This third source comes more from what each member of the group appears to be like as a person and less on what he or she says or does, although how he says what he says and how he does what he does also has a bearing on what he appears to be like as a person. The emphasis here is on what he appears to be, not on what he really is. For instance, certain persons in a group may appear to be like my mother, my father, my sister, my brother, or my boss without being any of those in fact. The important point is that I might therefore begin to relate to these particular people as though they were, indeed, my mother, father, sister, brother, or boss. I might like them or dislike them, or develop expectations of them, simply because I perceive them to be like other persons who were, or presently are, significant in my life. Also, I may be fully aware of having the same feelings toward them as I did, or presently do, toward important people in my life; or I may be only partly aware of the basis for these feelings; or, as is more frequently the case, I may have no awareness at all that I'm behaving toward these group members as I do for these reasons.

The technical word for such behavior is transference. We experience transference when the feelings, attitudes, and expectations we had toward persons who had special meaning for us earlier in our lives (such as close relatives) are transferred over to other persons who somehow resemble or remind us of the originals.

In individual psychotherapy the opportunity for transference to occur is naturally limited because there is only one other person, the therapist, in the patient's presence. The patient may perceive the therapist as good father, bad father, good mother, or bad mother and that's about it. Though other types of transference may develop, they arise much less frequently.

In the group situation, on the other hand, the presence of several different people each with their own characteristics provides the opportunity for multiple transference to come into play. When a patient recognizes that his relationship with someone is based largely or partly on transference he makes a valuable step forward. The realization may enable him to change that relationship into a more open, direct, and constructive one.

8.   A PERSON MAY EXPLORE AND PRACTICE NEW WAYS OF RELATING WITH OTHERS.

We learn most effectively by doing. A person in individual psychotherapy may gain some new understanding or awareness. However, within the confines of individual therapy the opportunity to put that new understanding or awareness into practice is severely limited. There is, after all, only one other person, the therapist, to practice on. Consequently the patient is forced almost immediately to do most of his practicing outside of the therapist's office. The therapist, in turn, must depend on the patient's report to learn what happened in the attempt. And the patient's report is invariably colored or distorted by his own perception of what took place.

In the group setting the patient can practice his new understanding and awareness with several different people, and he can do this in comparative safety and security. Later he can try out these new ways with people outside the group.

In this sense the group functions as a kind of sheltered workshop where patients can practice before moving to the "real" world.

There is an additional advantage for both the patient and the therapist. Here, in the group, the therapist can observe directly the patient's efforts. Thus both are relieved of the necessity of the patient having to report. Time is saved. Furthermore the evidence, being firsthand, is unquestionably reliable.

Many examples could be given. One of the most common is the person whose exchanges with others consists almost entirely of questions. He or she asks one question after another from everyone else present. This individual will even answer an inquiry with another question. Often he is not even aware of what he's doing, it's so automatic. Whatever his reasons may be the net effect is to make it difficult for others to get behind the person's questions to the person himself. When he is confronted with this behavior by the therapist or other members of the group, realizes that it is self-defeating and desires to change it, he can begin trying out the new way at once, dropping questions in favor of direct statements. The group is always there to remind him and to help him overcome the old habit.

Another common example is the man who first impresses the group as being a very agreeable person. He gets along well with everybody in the group, never sticks his neck out, never gets mad, never takes a risk. The group discovers he is in fact a highly compliant, submissive individual who just cannot assert himself under any circumstances. They point this out to him and encourage him to learn how to assert himself appropriately. Since he is still aiming to please, he probably agrees to try. However, the group doesn't forget and they won't let him forget. He may find it easier at first to go along with them. His efforts may be only halfhearted. However, as he begins to experience satisfaction in his training in self-assertion the effort becomes less pretending and increasingly real. Finally he is no longer a Casper Milquetoast. His practicing in the group has paid off.

9. WE CAN LEARN HOW OTHERS SEE US.

Do you remember asking yourself somewhere along the way as you were growing up, "I wonder what I really look like to other people. What kind of person do they think I am?" Perhaps you've had occasion to ask the question even more recently.

The natural answer is usually, "Well, I'll ask somebody." Okay. Then whom do you ask? That seems easy enough, so you cast about in your mind for someone you know to whom you can put the question. Who can give you an honest, objective, unbiased view of yourself? You consider one person, perhaps a close friend or relative, for a moment then dismiss him (or her) thinking well, yeah, he'll tell me straight up to a point but then he also has his own slant and after that I won't be able to believe too much of what he says. You consider a second person to ask and put him out of mind for the same reason; then a third and a fourth and a fifth until you run out of people who know you and wind up in surprise, feeling some distress and a little lonely in the realization that you know no one you can fully trust to give you a true picture of yourself.

The situation is different when you enter a group. Because group members have no established relationships with you outside the group, and therefore no special interests to influence them, they are free to give their impressions straight from the shoulder—or the hip, as the case may be. You can expect them to. Indeed, they're likely to do it without being asked! This holds true even in couples groups where both spouses are present. Although the spouse has a special interest, she is the only one who has and she is out-numbered by the others.

When the picture we get of ourselves from this kind of feedback is not what we would like it to be, the feedback in itself becomes a strong influence for change.

In individual therapy any feedback of this sort that a patient may get from his therapist, if it occurs at all, is much less. Furthermore, it is rarely as convincing as that which comes from a number of people who may differ as to age, sex, education, and so on.

10. THE GROUP STANDS FOR THE IDEAL FAM-ILY.

Frankly, I don't know if such a thing as an ideal family exists in real life. I do know that most of our patients come from families they see as far from ideal. Some of them, of course, have had no family at all. I'm confident, too, that a great many people who are not patients in treatment who have grown up in and out of families look back on their families with mixed feelings, some positive, some negative. With these people positive feelings usually outweigh the negative.

Particularly in mixed groups, meaning groups in which there are both men and women, group members after a time begin to feel as though the group were their family. Not the family they really had but the kind they had always wanted. It is in this sense that the group stands for the ideal family.

What do they mean by the ideal family? They certainly do not mean idyllic, that is to say, where an atmosphere of uninterrupted peace and contentment continues endlessly. This they don't expect.

On the contrary, they expect the ideal family to be very active, with a lot of give and take. Things would be happening. There wouldn't be anything dull about it. It would be alive and it would be warm. It would be a place where one could be one's own self, where one could be different, say male or female, without having to be like somebody else. One would not have to live up to someone else's expectations —like the expectations of one's parents, for example.

The ideal family would be a place one could count on to be there when it is needed, a place to come back to in difficult times. One could feel safe and secure there, knowing in one's heart that everybody in the family really cared for each other. That deep down people still cared even though they might have disagreements and arguments and differences of opinion. People in the family might fight among themselves, but that wouldn't be all of it—they would be tender and affectionate, too. It would be *my* family, where I belong, where there's a place for me no matter what. Sure, we might fight among ourselves—but don't let anybody else try it! Because then we stick together. And I would fight for each of them just as each one of them would fight for me, if it came to that.

That, briefly, seems to be the notions patients have of what an ideal family is like. Its quite unlike the family they remember growing up in.

But now, in the group, they discover the family they had wished for and dreamed of.

They can depend on the group. They can rely on it to meet regularly week after week at the same place. So it is stable over time and becomes an anchor point in time and space. This is reassuring. And there's a place in the group for each person, his own place. Here he can be different to the extent that he wants to be. Here he can be as open with himself and others as he can allow himself to be, secure in the knowledge that he will not be laughed at or humiliated. Although they may see things differently than he, they have his best interests at heart. He knows they care. He knows they try to understand. For him it's as close to an ideal family as he could hope for.

Hence the mere experience of being in an interactional group is in itself a corrective emotional experience. Indeed, Franz Alexander defines psychotherapy in just this way, a corrective emotional experience.*

The advantages of group therapy mentioned so far are largely advantages to the patient and for the patient. There remains one additional advantage which I am tempted to say is largely a benefit to the group leader or therapist. However, logic compels us to admit it is equally important to the group.

11. THE THERAPIST'S OWN DISTORTIONS ARE MINIMIZED.

We come to know the world in which we live through our several senses—seeing, hearing, touching, tasting, and so forth. We take the raw information we get from these senses and try to organize it in some way so as to get the meaning it carries. This process is what psychologists call perception.

Many factors influence perception. Fortunately, these factors are enough alike for each of us that we can and do perceive things pretty much the way others do. That is usually reassuring. If I hear bells and other people do, too, that's reassuring. On the other hand, exceptions to that general principle of perception can be disturbing. If I hear bells when nobody else does, that's disturbing—to say the least.

Our feelings, emotions, and attitudes influence the accu-

---

*Alexander, Franz. The dynamics of psychotherapy in the light of learning theory. American Journal of Psychiatry, 1963, 120, 440-448. This is essentially the same point of view expressed earlier by Frederick H. Allen of the Philadelphia Child Guidance Clinic when he spoke of psychotherapy as a living experience for the patient (*Psychotherapy with children*. New York, W. W. Norton & Co., 1942).

racy of our perceptions. Particularly our perceptions of other people and what they do, what they're up to. Sometimes the influence of our feelings, emotions, and attitudes is weak, sometimes strong. Sometimes our feelings, emotions, and attitudes allow us to see and understand people; sometimes our feelings, emotions, and attitudes prevent us from seeing and understanding people and events the way others do.

Slight differences in our perceptions from that of other people reflect our individual personalities. Because they are slight they are tolerable, and because they reflect our individualities they are probably desirable. Our contact with reality, with what is really going on, does not suffer when differences are small.

On the other hand, larger differences in the way we perceive from the way most others perceive can lead us astray. These larger differences result in twisting things around, more or less, in our own minds. When that occurs we are distorting reality, distorting what is really going on, and our contact with reality does suffer.

Although I speak of small differences and larger differences, obviously it's a matter of degree. The differences are only relatively small or large. Extremes, of course, are always easier to spot.

Psychotherapists, being human, are subject to the same laws of perception as everyone else. When they first come into training in psychotherapy their personal feelings, emotions, attitudes, and life experiences do influence the accuracy of their perceptions. They start out with their own hang-ups, special sensitivities, and blind spots. For this reason many psychotherapists in the course of their training obtain personal psychotherapy for themselves. Group therapists almost always do. They go into therapy groups as patients and learn from firsthand experience what it's like to be a patient in group therapy. They benefit from the experience just as others do.

When group therapists finish their training they are, as a result of having been in personal psychotherapy, better able to understand themselves. Consequently they are able to work with other people more smoothly and effectively. Their earlier hang-ups and blind spots are less likely to interfere in their relations with other persons. Nevertheless, some remnants of those old sensitivities and blind spots may still remain to crop up again. Therapists, also because of their training, are usually prepared for this possibility.

A psychotherapist who does individual psychotherapy, which by definition is where he is alone with a patient, may on occasion mishear, misperceive, or misunderstand his patient. Unless the therapist is being supervised, as in training situations, or is in close consultation with another therapist, these inaccuracies on his part are apt to go unnoticed. The effect is to slow down his patient's progress in treatment.

Most psychotherapists are interested in shortening rather than prolonging the course of treatment. They seek new ways and new methods to bring this about. When a therapist discovers that his patients are likely to move more rapidly in groups than in individual therapy because he himself makes fewer mistakes in groups he finds another good reason to prefer group therapy. He has learned he can rely on the group to call attention to any errors on his part. Provided, of course, he does not set himself up to be an authority beyond question. If the group is allowed to be spontaneous, if it is confident of its own freedom of give and take among its members, it will have little reluctance in questioning the therapist when it feels he is inaccurate in what he sees or hears.

You can always use the group to check your perceptions

of other persons in the group or of what is taking place in the group. You can do this whether you happen to be a patient or client in the group or whether you happen to be the therapist or leader in the group. Here the majority, call it the consensus, prevails. And the majority or consensus can work in either direction. It can agree with you or disagree with you. If one person takes exception to what you think you have heard or seen, the probability that he is the one who is misperceiving is equal to the probability that you are the one who is misperceiving. However, if several members concur, stop and take heed. You may still be correct, but the chances are less and less likely that you are.

VI

Pitfalls

Certain situations arise in the course of group sessions that present special difficulties or dilemmas. If you are already leading groups you know they occur. If you are going to lead groups you will want to know what they are before they happen. Being forewarned is being forearmed.

The most common pitfalls have to do with silences, religion, questions, the distinction between management and psychotherapy, and misuse of the group.

Silences

There are all sorts of silences. Silences on the part of individuals in the group, silences on the part of the group as a whole. The meaning of individual silences will be determined just as they are in individual therapy. Group silences are somewhat different to deal with.

Leaders and therapists are apt to become anxious and tense when their groups lapse into silence. Perhaps more so than at other times in their work with patients. Understanding the meaning of the silence will help you to handle it.

First of all, realize that silences affect your patients as much as silences affect you. Your patients can become every bit as anxious and tense by a silence as you do. Now usually, though not always, the most anxious person will be the first to break the silence. If you know this, you can hold on to your anxiety and wait it out, confident that sooner or later someone in the group will find the silence so unbearable he will say something to break it. Of course he doesn't know this, but you do. And this puts you ahead.

I said usually, though not always, the most anxious person in the group will be the first to break the silence because the most anxious person may find himself paralyzed into speechlessness by the anxiety the silence creates. In this case the silence will be broken by the next most anxious person in the group, perhaps the one who becomes talkative when he's tense and anxious. The result is the same as far as you're concerned—you're relieved of the need to break the silence yourself.

This is one way to handle a silence. It is also a hard way, both for the therapist and for the group. An easier and rather more natural solution would be for you to observe aloud to the group what you feel at the moment. For example, "This silence bothers me. I can feel the tension among us." That's all, no questions, no interpretations added. Let the members of the group pick up and respond. Or you might say, "I wonder where we're at."

Note the language. ". . . the tension among *us*," rather than the tension *in the group,* and ". . . where *we're* at," rather than where *you're* at. Include yourself in. If you see yourself to be an important part of this group, let your language reflect it. Your language will reveal you, one way or the other. If you do not want to be considered part of this group, if you feel a distinction and want to remain apart (apart, not part), then the use of "you" or "the group" instead of "we" or "us" will make it clear that there is a division between you and the members of the group. In that sense you let it be known that you don't really belong even if you are the therapist or leader. Whether you realize it or not, it's a put-down. Your language speaks for you.

Patients, especially in groups and especially in groups

just starting out, may become silent almost deliberately in a kind of set-up operation. It's as though they know that nature abhors a vacuum, so they proceed to set one up in the hope that the leader will rush in to fill it. It's one of their ways to get him to move, to take over active direction of the group. When it works it's very effective in getting them what they want. For when the leader once falls for the trap the group sees that it works and will try it again. Then the silences come again and again until pretty soon the leader or therapist finds himself doing most of the talking. At this point he might feel he'd been taken, somehow, without knowing quite how.

If you become aware that this is happening to you, you can handle it as mentioned before by observing aloud to the group what you feel is going on. Be brief, then stop. They'll get the message—that you don't intend to do their work for them.

There are other types of silences. Not all are negative. Some are constructive and useful. You will have to be tuned in to the group to recognize each one for what it is. For example, the group may become quiet because of some deeply moving experience that has just taken place. They are now meditating on it, joined together in silence. Such a silence serves to bring the group closer together. Do not attempt to interrupt it. It will end naturally.

Religion

Religion is a particularly touchy subject. People are apt to feel pretty strongly about religion, one way or another. So what do we do when it comes up in a therapy group? Are there any guidelines to assist us?

Yes, there are. First, psychotherapists in general adhere to the principle that we do not impose our own personal values or beliefs on our patients. To do so would be to take unfair advantage of them, for one thing. Religion is simply one area in which the principle operates. Therefore we deliberately avoid doing anything to influence patients in the direction of our own personal religious beliefs. Not always an easy thing to do, yet we must try. Think what a horrid thing it would be to fashion our patients into images of ourselves! Even if we could. I have known a few—very few, fortunately —therapists in training who were convinced that if they could persuade their patients to lead their lives as the therapist led his, religion and all, the patient would have it made. These therapists learned better as they went along—thank God!

Second, as psychotherapists religion is not our business. We deal with the natural world, not the supernatural. Even ministers, priests, and rabbis who are trained in psychotherapy and engage in group therapy know enough to switch hats when they do. You can play one or the other but not both at the same time. Keep in mind which ball park you are in.

With these thoughts in mind, what do we do when someone in the group wants to talk about religion? First we listen to try to understand what he is getting at. If we find he wants information, about religious practices or a particular church or denomination, he's encouraged to seek the appropriate professional sources to supply it. This he can do outside of the group.

However, if what he wants is to vent his feelings about religion, then let him do so. Listen to him in the same way you would listen if he were expressing his feelings about his boss, his teacher, his coach, his parents, the establishment, or whatever. Usually these are strongly negative feelings at first and he needs to get them out, to ventilate. Give him that opportunity. You don't have to debate it with him and you don't need to defend the church. The church can take care of itself well enough. He will probably feel better when he gets his feelings off his chest. Then he'll be able to drop the matter and go on to give his attention to what is happening closer at hand in the group. Others in the group are not likely to be drawn into an argument with him. They are apt to understand that he is trying to get something out of his system and will allow him to so they can all move on.

Often a patient will report to the group that he has started back to church again. Take it as evidence that the patient feels better about himself, about being with other people, and about the church itself. In other words, he can now tolerate a situation which before he found too painful to bear. He is improving. Give him the satisfaction of your acknowledgment of it.

Questions, Questions, Questions

Not every question requires an answer. However, every question requires that you listen intently. For questions can be very revealing—of the person asking them.

As there are several kinds of silences, so there are several kinds of questions.

The kind we are most familiar with, of course, is the one where the questioner honestly desires information of some sort. When we hear a question of this kind we feel almost compelled to answer. That is natural enough in everyday life and entirely appropriate. What happens, however, is that we almost automatically begin to react to all questions as though they were all of this sort, honestly asking for information, and we feel the same compulsion to answer. This is the point at which we have to watch ourselves. For the person asking the question may not really want information. He may want to accomplish something else with his question. He may intend his question to serve some other purpose.

His question may be for effect only. He doesn't expect an answer. In English literature and composition this is known as a rhetorical question. Orators like to use it in speeches. Perhaps the most famous example, familiar to people who have taken Latin in school, is Cicero's opening line in a speech to the Senate and people of Rome: "How long, O Cataline, will you continue to abuse our patience?"

Then there is the question which is put only to show how much the person knows who asks the question. Anyone who has ever been in a class with other students knows this one. The questioner is showing off, and everyone is aware of it. He may also be trying to put down his teacher. This, too, is usually pretty obvious.

Another kind of question is the question which comes as a reply to a question. "Do you love your husband?" "Well, what do you think?" Evasion, pure and simple. Even when a therapist resorts to it. "Doctor, am I getting better?" Doctor: "What do you think?" One experiences an immediate feeling of frustration followed by ill-suppressed anger in either case.

Now that you are thinking about it other kinds of questions will probably come to mind. The kind that serves as a delaying tactic, for example. Every student, and every child, knows that one. Keep teacher, or mom or dad, busy so as not to reach the next point on the agenda, whether it's a test, or going to bed, or arriving at a decision of some sort.

Persons in groups are constantly asking questions of each other. Such questions can be valuable to the group leader once he recognizes that often the questioner discloses in his question his own concern, his own special perception of what is going on. These questions become a form of projection in the sense of externalizing one's inner private world. They are apt to be found where the questioner takes the attitude of trying to be helpful. He can only be helpful and understanding by drawing on his own life experiences, of course, and so he unwittingly reveals himself. If a person in the group is weeping silently, person B might ask, "Are you scared?" because B is inclined to cry when she is frightened. Person C might ask, "Are you angry?" because C is likely to cry when she is angry. They have both discovered that grief and sorrow are not the only reasons for tears.

Some persons who are trying to work as psychotherapists have fallen into the habit of asking question after question after question of their patients. These therapists are the less experienced ones who may still be very early in their careers. They commonly like to describe their approach as the "common sense" method of psychotherapy. It might better be called the Socratic method after Socrates in ancient Greece who put questions to his students as a way of leading them to think and to learn. It may be great for head work where one learns to use reason, logic, and inference. But we are dealing with feelings, attitudes, and emotions. No wonder then that the question after question method becomes dull, boring, lifeless, and relatively ineffective. And the therapist remains as safely hidden behind his questions as patients are hidden behind theirs.

Are there any honest, legitimate questions a therapist or leader may ask? Indeed there are. When a therapist is trying to grasp and understand what a patient is trying to express, it is entirely appropriate for the therapist to inquire whether he (the therapist) is on the right track. "You feel that your husband let you down, is that it?" Such questions often help the patient to clarify his feelings in his own mind. Therefore they are therapeutically useful. They are distinct from probing, digging questions, which are generally not very useful. They are also distinct from interpretive questions, questions put by the therapist to help the patient to see the connection between feelings and events so as to achieve insight. Insight has proven to be of limited value because it is mostly head work, having little to do with feelings and attitudes.

If you are working as a psychotherapist you are bound to ask questions. Just be prudent and know what you are up to. As a guide, if you find you are bored, if you find you are asking so many questions that you wind up doing most of the talking during a session, then stop and take stock. You're in a rut. Or you've been trapped.

Management vs. Psychotherapy

Physicians and social case workers are apt to get hung up on this one.

Physicians who are psychiatrists are particularly prone to have trouble keeping in mind the difference between management and psychotherapy. This is understandable since psychiatrists are physicians first. As physicians they are trained to do *for* their patients, to take responsibility for them. And in certain aspects of their work as psychiatrists they continue to do so. And quite properly and appropriately so. For example, when a psychiatrist prescribes medication or applies shock therapy or any of the physical therapies he is involved in management of his patient and assumes the same responsibility for his management of the patient as, say, a physician who is a surgeon would assume for the operative management of his patient in surgery.

Difficulty arises, however, for the psychiatrist when he switches from other forms of treatment to psychotherapy as the treatment. For in other forms of treatment the psychiatrist retains responsibility for the patient, while in psychotherapy the psychiatrist must shift gears to allow responsibility to rest with the patient. A therapist does not attempt to "manage" his patient's life, to take responsibility for it. He will help the patient to clarify his (the patient's) feelings, to see the options open to him, and to choose among them the one the patient sees to be in his own best interest. But a competent therapist does not make his patient's decisions for him. Nor does he give him advice as to how to lead his life.

From the other end of the stick, from the patient's point of view this turnaround in what his psychiatrist is doing must be rather puzzling, too. I don't know whether any psychiatrist has ever said outright to a patient, "I will manage your medication but I won't manage your life." However, I do know many psychiatrists, who are primarily psychotherapists, who make it a rule not to prescribe medication for any of their patients. One reason for the rule is to avoid this management vs. psychotherapy confusion. Another reason, related to the first, is to forestall the possibility of the patient developing a sense of dependency either on the doctor or on the medicine.

Social workers run into the same difficulty. In many aspects of their work they, too, assume responsibility for their clients, do for them, and offer advice and counsel. They too, therefore, find it hard to shift gears when they move into psychotherapy with their clients. Yet the principle holds: in psychotherapy responsibility for his life rests with the patient. The therapist's only responsibility is a professional one—to be an effective therapist.

Misuse of the Group

In their training psychotherapists learn they are not to take advantage of their patients. The principle is a sound one, of course. Everybody agrees on it. Generally it's a matter of ethics which nobody disputes. Although application of the principle in most situations is clear enough, its application in one area is not so clear. This is in the area of psychotherapy where the principle translates into a directive which states that a therapist is not to use his patients for his own personal therapy.

It follows that if a therapist wants the benefits of personal psychotherapy for himself, as many do, he should seek it elsewhere than from his patients. In other words, he should select a therapist of his own and enter treatment as a patient of that therapist. Or he might enter a therapy group led by another group therapist. Indeed, this happens to be a common practice among group therapists.

All this seems straightforward enough. What's the rub?

Well, many psychotherapists in their training nowadays are also taught that it is all right to be human, genuine, warm, and open with a patient. Therapists who are psychoanalysts do not go along with this, of course. They believe the analyst should continue to remain relatively cool and detached with a patient. Many young therapists who are turned off by this psychoanalytic attitude find a greater attraction in those therapeutic approaches which permit the therapist to interact honestly with his patient as one human being to another. And that is where the rub comes in: how can a therapist relate to a patient in this manner without slipping into the error of using the relationship for his own benefit as a kind of psychotherapy?

If you find yourself in this squeeze, take heart. There is a way to keep your head clear and know what you're about. With your patient, or patients in your therapy group, be as open and honest with your feelings as it is possible and comfortable for you to be under the circumstances—provided you stay in the here and now of what is taking place. Pay attention to your feelings and discover how to use them to keep in touch with what is going on. As long as you stay with the present it won't be personal therapy for you, in the usual sense. However, it does become personal therapy for you the moment you allow yourself to search for the origin of your feeling or attitude in your past life history. Do not use your patient's time for this. Unless, of course, you are willing to reimburse your patient for his time as your therapist.

So keep in mind that as long as you avoid using the group's time to trace the origins of your own feelings and attitudes you are not misusing the group. Other than that, allow yourself to be as much a part of the group as you can comfortably manage to be. You do want to be in touch with what is happening, to be a live and living participant in meaningful change for them. When you do this you'll find you are changing, too. That is because your life is becoming richer as a result of your relationship with your patients. Take satisfaction in it. It's part of your reward as a psychotherapist. No need to feel guilty about this kind of experience for it is not personal therapy for you. What it is, is personal and professional growth.

VII

Who Comes In—and How

As was stated earlier, it makes a difference whether a group is education oriented (the small group field) or treatment oriented (group psychotherapy). One aspect of the difference is seen in who comes in to the group, and in how he comes in.

If you are interested in entering one of the groups within the small group field—a sensitivity training group, a training lab, a T-group, an encounter group, a self-growth or self-enhancement group, and the like—you will find you can do so easily. All comers are welcome. Provided you have the money, of course. And provided the group hasn't reached its size limit. This is not too likely to occur, however, since it will usually accommodate from fifteen to fifty people, and if applications go over the limit the leaders stand ready to open a second group rather than disappoint anyone and turn away business. For the leaders (trainers, facilitators, change agents) of such groups generally think of themselves as being in a business, a business in the service of education, it is true, but a business nevertheless. The public usually does not notice this side of it. What the public sees is an educational enterprise.

The educational system the public is familiar with is a system that is open to everyone. If he can afford it. The small group field fits that image. Although a person sometimes has to fulfill certain requirements before being allowed to enroll in a course in school, in the small group field this is more the exception than the rule. Usually there is no screening whatever, so you don't need to worry about being screened out. Just send in your application along with your registration fee and show up at the right time and place.

Not so in group therapy. Although you may be unaware of any requirements for entering a therapy group, the group therapist is very much aware of them.

One requirement which almost all group therapists agree upon is that you recognize that you are emotionally troubled and that you are therefore coming for treatment, whether you think of yourself as a patient or not. Emotionally troubled doesn't mean crazy. You can be emotionally troubled without being crazy in the least.

Beyond that one requirement different therapists look for different things.

The more disturbed a person is the more he has to do to get back to his old self. The young adult who has been strung out on drugs for three weeks is farther from his usual self than is the young adult who gets a headache any time his father says something disagreeable. By the same token, the less disturbed a person is the less work he has to do in therapy. Likewise, a therapist will get better results more rapidly with less disturbed patients than with more disturbed patients, either in individual therapy or in group therapy. If a therapist wants the satisfaction of seeing more positive results in return for his efforts he need only play the percentages and work with the less disturbed patients to begin with. Therapists, particularly those just starting out, need to know their work is useful and that they are truly effective. Otherwise they would be justified in giving it up and turning to some other occupation.

Translated into practice this means, if you are a therapist, that you will be on solid ground when you accept as patients only those persons whom you tend to like and feel you can work with profitably with some reasonable chance of success. You are not obliged to take on everybody. There are other therapists around to share the load. After all, the time you share with your patient is part of your life, too. You have a right to feel it is being well spent.

I use two additional requirements to determine whether a patient qualifies for group therapy. Neither is based on diagnosis, the official label for what is wrong with him, though both do have implications for the diagnostic status of the individual.

The first requirement is motivation: it must be positive. This means that a person has to show that he is ready and willing to do something in his own behalf. He needs to want to do whatever it may be necessary for him to do to regain the freedom within himself to live a useful and satisfying life. It is important that this is what he wants for himself— not what somebody else wants for him. If he is coming because someone else has pressured him into coming the likelihood that he will gain anything of value for himself is dim. If a man asks for group therapy because a judge gave him the choice of seeking psychotherapy or going to jail, that man feels pressured into coming and will probably spend his time in therapy as he would spend it in jail—doing nothing. If a woman comes because her husband insists that she's the one who needs help, nothing very constructive is likely to happen with her either.

I have found this first requirement to be so highly related to the successful outcome of therapy that I will accept as patients in individual therapy or in group therapy only persons who convince me that their motivation for coming is positive and genuine. Otherwise we are wasting our time, theirs and mine alike.

How do we know when a person is well motivated? There are some simple and easy ways to check it out. If the person is a mother with small children at home, is she willing to arrange for a baby-sitter? If so, she's probably well motivated. Is the man who is employed full-time willing to arrange to get time off to come? If so, he is probably well motivated. Does the person have to arrange for transportation or travel some distance to come? If so, he or she is probably well motivated. In each case the person must exert himself in some special way to demonstrate his motivation. Persons who are not properly motivated are apt to feel the extra effort is just too much and will quickly lose interest.

Isn't a person's willingness to pay for these professional services an indication in itself of proper motivation? To some extent, yes. Money is important to many people, particularly if they have had to work hard for what they've got. For them, willingness to pay for the services will be some indication of adequate motivation. However, willingness to pay is not a completely reliable test of motivation for the reason that many people also use money to get themselves off the hook, to relieve them of any meaningful involvement with others. Their attitude seems to be, "I've paid my dues, and that's enough. That's all you'll get out of me." And sure enough, they are right. You can expect them to pay their "dues" for a few sessions and then drop out without a word to anybody.

The requirement of positive motivation operates to rule out persons who fall into two diagnostic categories. One is the category of addictions to alcohol and other drugs. But remember that many people drink who cannot by any stretch of the imagination be called addicted. Strictly social drinkers are not addicts, therefore their motivation for psychotherapy is not lessened because of their drinking. However, confirmed alcoholics and other drug addicts are difficult to deal with in ordinary groups.

The second category of persons ruled out on the basis of motivation are those classed as behavior disorders, character disorders, sociopaths or psychopaths. These all mean about the same thing. They are people who do not seem to learn from experience, who do not form close and lasting attachments, who seek immediate gratification of their needs, and who seem to be bent on self-destruction one way or another. These people almost never develop a sense of belonging in a therapy group. And without that sense of belonging, of identification, to begin with such a person will remain untouched by the group, sabotage all the group's efforts to establish some meaningful relationships with him, and finally leave as he came, nothing accomplished.

My second requirement of a person being considered for group therapy has to do with communicability: he should be able to communicate with others pretty much in normal fashion. This is simply a matter of being able to talk with others in such a way that they will understand what he is saying. And in like manner, it is his ability in turn to understand what others are saying. It is his capacity to carry on an ordinary conversation.

Perhaps you've taken it for granted that everybody can communicate in this way. If so, you may be a little surprised that I mention it. Let me explain.

One indication of severe emotional disorder is the breakdown of a person's ability to communicate. He may become incoherent. Or he may develop a special language of his own and speak in a kind of code. Without a key to the code you would have no idea what he was saying. This breakdown in ability to communicate is a characteristic feature of many of the psychoses. Consequently the requirement of ability to communicate tends to screen out people in one diagnostic category, persons classed as psychotic.

This requirement also rules out one other, and rather more obvious, type of person. He is the one with a hearing impairment. People who are hard of hearing find difficulty in following a conversation among two or more people. They begin to feel themselves to be on the fringe of the group at first, then this gives way to a feeling of being left out completely. The experience is distressing. It is definitely not therapeutic and we do the person an injustice by bringing him into the group.

It may have occurred to you that many elderly persons tend to be hard of hearing. This is true. The requirement affects them, too. Elderly persons do as well as others in group therapy provided there's no hearing loss. When there is, they don't.

We have looked at who comes in. You can see that the great majority of people qualify. Only a relatively few don't.

Now let's look at how they come in.

You are a group therapist and you are considering a patient who has been referred to you for group therapy. This is your first meeting with him. As the interview moves along you gain a favorable impression of him with the feeling that you might be able to work well together. In your mind you have checked him out with respect to his motivation for seeking psychotherapy and his ability to communicate. You are reasonably satisfied he qualifies on both counts. Overall he strikes you as being a good prospect for group therapy. What then?

First, tell him something about the group. He has a right to have some idea of what he's getting into. I like to start by asking him what he knows about group therapy or what he's heard about it. People have all sorts of ideas about it. Some may even have been in a group before. Here is an opportunity for you to clear up any misconceptions he might have or to point out how your group will be different from ones he has been in.

In describing your group it is well to mention its size; whether it is a mixed group of men and women or has only men or only women; how often it meets each week, and how long each session lasts.

This is the time to discuss the matter of confidentiality, too, and you might make it clear to him that everybody in the group agrees to keep in strictest confidence anything that goes on in the group. He is generally relieved to know this and will say so, adding that he realizes no one in the group would be able to speak freely without such assurance. I then like to anticipate with the patient the occasional time ahead when he will want to talk about the group to someone who is not in it, perhaps his wife or close friend. From my point of view it is all right for him to do so *provided he mentions no names,* which is the real key to confidentiality.

You will also want to explain to him the importance of regular attendance. Your group may observe special rules in this regard. For example, some groups operate with the understanding that if any person misses three sessions in a row without notifying the leader then that person is automatically dropped from the group.

There may be other special ground rules or procedures he should know about. One I have found quite useful deals with a new patient's hesitation to commit himself to something unknown, on the one hand, and his acceptance by the group on the other. It is our custom in the group for the newcomer to attend three sessions to discover for himself what the group is like. He can expect me to ask him toward the end of the third session how he feels about going on with the group. He is also told that he can expect me to ask the other members of the group how they feel about having him go on with them.

Clearly it is a two-way proposition. Everybody has a chance to express their feelings. This is one of the beauties of the procedure. Do not lose this opportunity for people to express themselves by allowing the patients to avoid saying how they feel about the newcomer. Some will try to avoid the issue by turning the question into a vote and giving a bare yes or no answer. Don't let them get away with it. Encourage them to come forth with what they really feel.

A group does not often turn down a newcomer, though it may on rare occasions. When it does the procedure is still constructive because everything takes place in the open. There is no secret ballot, nothing is hidden. The rejected newcomer knows what's happening and why it's happening. There is no vacuum for him to fill with his own fantasies. I remember one patient who came into a group because he was making a mess of his life. He was drinking more than he should, for one thing, and he knew it. During his first session with the group it was apparent to all that he'd been drinking. They took notice but let it pass. At the next session he came in half an hour late and tighter than before. At the third session he was drunk enough to be disruptive, interrupting what people were saying, and ignoring what was going on. When he was asked whether he cared to continue in the group it was almost impossible to make out whether he said yes or no. But the group knew how they felt about him and told him so in no uncertain terms. They were concerned about him and as kind as they could be. Nevertheless, they let him know that he was obviously not very serious about coming to group and that they were not going to allow him to waste their time and money. They were sorry, truly, but that's the way it was. And he left, knowing full well the reasons why he had been turned down.

So far in this initial interview the matter of fees has not been touched on. I prefer to put this last and take it up when other things have been settled.

By now the prospective patient has been filled in with the information he needs to have about the group. If he has had any questions along the way he will have asked them and they will have been answered. You have accomplished the first step of the initial interview, of informing the newcomer about the group.

The next step is to invite the prospective patient to meet with the group. "Invite" and "meet" are two important words here. You *invite* him into the group in a real sense: it is a genuine invitation, one which he is free to accept or decline. He makes the decision. You want him of his own free will, remember, without pressure from you or anyone else although your attitude makes it clear that you will welcome him. If he decides against it, accept his decision. And you invite him to "meet" with the group rather than join it outright because you won't know until near the end of the third session whether the group will accept him.

In many instances the person considering entering a group experiences mixed feelings—he wants to come in and he doesn't want to come in. Mostly he is scared. The thought of being with a group of total strangers is too much. How can one talk about personal matters with strangers? The apprehension and anxiety he feels are almost paralyzing. It is usually best to recognize this state and avoid trying to force the issue by false assurances. What he needs is to have one person in the group who is not a stranger to him. That person would be you as the therapist. And the way to help him overcome the feeling that you, too, are a stranger is to arrange to see him in individual interviews a few times before he comes to a group session. After he has seen you a few times in individual therapy he may be ready to venture into the group—provided you'll be there when he comes. For you have become a bridge for him, a bridge from outside to inside.

Once inside, anything can happen. Very often people who swear up and down they won't be able to say a word in the group find themselves becoming quite talkative half-way through the first group session. As is usually the case, the unknown is frightening. The reality isn't.

To summarize, persons qualify for admission into therapy groups on two points. One is ability to communicate, the other is positive motivation. Ability to communicate tends to rule out persons with severe emotional disturbance (psychosis) and persons who are hard of hearing. Positive motivation tends to rule out persons who have been pressured into coming in the first place; and addicts, either drug or alcohol. Thus we see who comes into therapy groups. How they come in follows two steps. The first step consists of describing to the prospective patient what the group is like and, in a general way, how it operates. The second step is an invitation to the prospective member to come into the group. It sometimes becomes necessary to see the prospective member a few times in individual psychotherapy before introducing him into the group.

What about the group itself, is it readied in some way to receive a newcomer? Yes, it is. But vaguely, not specifically. The vagueness is deliberate.

Sometimes, usually when the group has fallen below its normal size in numbers, members will ask the therapist whether he's going to bring another person into the group. In a sense they're rather like children asking for a baby brother or sister. The experienced therapist will say yes, of course, because he too wants to bring the group back to normal size. But he will also then proceed to take advantage of this opportunity to encourage the group to indulge in their fantasies about this as yet unknown person. What kind of an addition to their group would they like to have? Man, woman? Black, white? Young, old? Again, it's as though mother were pregnant and everybody's expecting—but who knows what the unborn child will turn out to be like? They can only fantasize and thus reveal their needs and wishes.

VIII

Special Concerns: Suicide

In the course of his practice a group therapist must deal with a variety of concerns. Many are so specific to an individual in the group or to the situation or to an event taking place that he will have to handle them pretty much as they occur, almost as though he were ad-libbing—even though we know his ad-libbing is not random because it is based on years of training. However, two of these concerns stand out as deserving of attention before they crop up because unless the therapist is prepared he is unlikely on the spur of the moment to deal effectively with them.

Suicide is the first of the two. Properly speaking, we should say *thoughts* of suicide since actual suicide, fortunately, happens only once in a great while in group therapy. But thoughts of suicide are very common. So the therapist needs to know what to make of ideas of self-destruction.

If there is one common denominator among the persons who come into group therapy it is depression. People are down in mood, low in morale, squeezed by life, generally unhappy. It's a miserable state to be in. Indeed, everybody wants out of it. And one way out is to die. Obviously, death does put an end to suffering. I sometimes wonder whether there is anybody in this world who has lived through any real hardships in life who has not thought of death at one time or another as a way to end it all.

Death is known to be one of the tabooed topics in our civilization. People avoid talking about it if at all possible.

Just as they avoid talking about sex openly and matter-of-factly. Of course suicide, as a form of death, is also taboo as a topic of conversation. And have you ever noticed that when death or suicide or sex does come up in conversation it's apt to be someone else's death or suicide attempt or sex life and not our own?

Yes, one of the conditions of human existence is death. That being the case, one would expect man as a rational, logical, reasoning creature to give death due consideration. We don't, though. We try to ignore it as any concern of our own. How many people do you know who have made the necessary final arrangements? Most of us keep putting it off. In fact, so many of us keep putting out of mind any thoughts of our own death that not thinking about death is taken to be normal—and even healthy. The strange thing is that those who do give it close thought are often considered to be hypochondriacs, "crocks." Granted, of course, that when the thought of death bugs them to the point they can think of little else and can get little or no sleep then they are, in truth, hypochondriac.

The group therapist knows about hypochondriacs. He knows they fear death, fear they will die in a short time, and do not want to die. Hence although they talk about death and dying they are not a suicidal risk. That's the last thing they want!

The therapist will hear his patients in groups admit in their despair to thoughts of doing away with themselves. What does he make of it? Certainly he doesn't want to lose anyone. Then how does he evaluate the risk, the likelihood of someone making the attempt and succeeding?

The experienced therapist knows to listen carefully and intently, yet without displaying alarm or panic. He is careful of his own reaction for two good reasons.

In the first place, patients in the group are likely to get uptight when they hear one of the group talk about committing suicide. They won't know how to react. In this predicament they will glance at the therapist for some cue. How is he dealing with it? If he is matter-of-fact, that's their cue and they will be matter-of-fact, too. If he is alarmed, that is their cue and they will be alarmed, too. He is a "lead-er" in the very real sense of providing them with leads.

In the second place, the person who mentions to the group that he is thinking about doing away with himself is also keenly aware of the therapist's reaction. Of course, the patient is aware of how the others are taking it, too, but they don't have the same importance to him at this moment. For when the therapist remains calm as he hears the patient, the patient feels reassured. Feeling reassured and safe, he can go on to speak of what's bothering him. By contrast, when the therapist shows alarm even by his facial expression the patient is apt to think to himself, "Good grief! If he is alarmed I must really be in bad shape." And whatever remaining bit of confidence he has left begins to falter. No therapist wants to allow that to happen.

Yet the leader must assess the level of risk the patient presents at this point. Now as ever he retains professional responsibility for taking appropriate action when necessary to safeguard the patient's life. This calls for good clinical judgment.

You can recognize three levels of risk with the person who contemplates suicide. At the first level he is thinking about it. At the second level he is threatening to do it. And at the third level he makes an actual attempt at it.

If everybody who ever thought of suicide actually made a successful attempt at it, the populations of the countries of our Western civilization would be greatly reduced by now.

Fortunately, thoughts of suicide do not necessarily lead on to attempts at suicide. This does not mean, however, that we should take talk of suicide lightly. That would be a mistake. Suicide, even at the level of just thinking about it, is serious business.

People who talk of suicide are talking out of their depression. When a depression deepens the likelihood of suicide increases. Therefore the depth of a depression ties in with the three levels of risk. There are ways of gauging the depth of a depression and, hence, the level of risk.

Almost everyone knows what it is like to feel low at one time or another. When our spirits are down and our mood is blue we lose our appetite. We'll miss a meal and hardly notice it. We're in no mood for sex, either. And our sleep is likely to be troubled and disturbed, not restful. This may go on for a day or two and then things change, our spirits lift, our mood is brighter, our appetite returns, we can enjoy sex again, and get a good night's sleep. This happens so frequently to so many people it has to be considered normal. People hardly ever think of suicide at these times.

When those symptoms go on beyond a very few days the person enters the first stage of a clinical depression. As a result of his loss of appetite he begins to lose weight. He not only loses interest in food, he loses interest in sex as well. Indeed, he loses interest in just about everything and everybody. His relations with other persons begin to suffer. His work suffers. He begins to have trouble getting off to sleep and when he wakes in the morning he doesn't feel refreshed or rested. It's as though everything about him has slowed down. At this stage he will think of suicide. Even if he doesn't talk about it you can be pretty sure he is thinking about it just the same.

In the next stage the depression continues and gets worse.

The loss of weight is easily apparent. The patient may complain of constipation and headaches. He is droopy. He broods. He looks like he is miserable. It is an effort for him to do anything. The world appears colorless and tasteless to him. He cannot get a decent night's sleep. It begins to seem to him that he will never be able to shake off his depression. Life has become too much of a burden to continue. He's been thinking suicide; now he threatens to do it.

This indicates the second level of risk. The therapist may still hesitate to suggest that the patient be hospitalized, however, because of the advantage to both the patient and the group to keep him out of the hospital as long as possible.

Often just the thought of the group is enough to keep a patient from carrying out his threats of self-destruction. Provided, of course, he has really become a part of the group. Otherwise the thought of the group won't matter much. I remember one patient, a woman in this instance, who came into group one day and said, "You know, I almost didn't make it back here today. The day before yesterday I'd gotten into it with my husband, we had a big fight and I was pretty upset. So I had a couple of drinks, got in my car, and was headed down the highway to Benton at a pretty good speed. And I thought how easy it would be to swerve into one of those concrete piers near those overpasses. And I damn near did. I sure wanted to. Then I thought, what would the group say? And that stopped me." With that, she burst into tears.

Experienced therapists frequently resort to another tactic to tide them over with a patient who is in the second stage of depression, at the second level of risk. The tactic depends entirely on the relationship between therapist and patient. It must be positive, genuine, warm, and firm. When the relationship is like this the therapist can ask the patient who threatens to commit suicide to agree to get in touch with him (the therapist) before he makes any definite move in that direction. If the patient agrees, the therapist can breathe easier.

A note of caution is due here. Leaders who are trained only in Transactional Analysis (T.A.) or who rely exclusively on the T.A. approach tend to become mechanical with patients. T.A. people speak in terms of contracts, a highly popular word with them. Consequently, they will often in their very first meeting with him, try to obtain a contract from the patient threatening suicide that he will not kill himself. This is like asking the patient rather mechanically to promise not to commit suicide and, because it ignores the relationship between them, the procedure is likely to fall flat and the patient refuses. If you are a T.A. person, check your relationship with your patient if you want your use of contracts in this regard to be effective.

In the third stage of depression, where the greatest level of risk exists, the patient may be expected to attempt to kill himself. Now he not only lies awake for a long time before dropping off to sleep, he also wakes up in the early morning hours between 1:00 and 3:00 and has trouble getting back to sleep. The house is still, everybody is asleep, he feels completely alone. This is the time when most suicides occur. There is nobody to stop him.

When your depressed patient reports that he has been waking up in those early morning hours it is your cue to take action. See to it that a relative or friend is made aware of the hazard and will remain with the patient at all times, or have the patient admitted to a hospital. This is no time to take chances.

An equally important cue at this point is furnished by the patient who lets you know, directly or indirectly, that he is putting his affairs in order. Take it seriously. He is close to suicide.

Inexperienced psychotherapists are sometimes fooled by a deeply despondent patient whose depression seems suddenly to have lifted. The person seems bright again, perhaps almost cheerful. His step is lighter, as though a burden has been lifted from his shoulders. He seems at peace with himself. No, he's not trying deliberately to fool you. He does feel better—but not for the reasons you think, if you're thinking he is over his depression. He feels better because he has reached a decision. It is the same kind of relief one feels on arriving at any decision, no matter what. Only in this case the decision is actually to kill himself. So don't allow yourself to be caught off guard. The healthy way for a depression to lift is gradually and slowly, over days and weeks.

Many people commit suicide who are not clinically depressed. That is to say, they give no outward signs of despondency and you could not tell they are depressed by any objective evidence, except, perhaps, that they have put their affairs in order and have made final arrangements. These people will not admit to others that they have reached the end of their rope. They are accustomed to handling things themselves, in their own way. They won't seek help. For that reason you won't find them in psychotherapy of any sort, including group therapy.

Now, since obviously sooner or later every living person dies, once in a while death will strike a member of your group. Even the therapist is not immune. Heart attacks are common enough and people die from other illnesses as well. What do you do when one of your group does die?

Have your session as scheduled. By no means postpone it. At this time the group has a special need to be together. They have many feelings to share, many feelings to explore. Don't allow them to get sidetracked. You may expect shock, and grief, and sadness. But look for guilt and resentment, too. Let it all come out. Death is death, whether it occurs by natural causes or by suicide. Encourage the group to face it with all of its possible ramifications at the moment. They will be in a better position to deal with it next time death comes to someone in their lives. In this sense the group session following the death of a member can be especially therapeutic.

On rare occasions the group may be shaken by the death of a person who had never been a member of the group at all. The assassination of President Kennedy was such a time. I am aware of at least five therapy groups that devoted their next session entirely to their feelings about it, and I would guess the same thing was happening to other groups around the country. The sense of personal loss, of shock and outrage was too intense to dismiss. Though death separates, it also brings people together.

To summarize, you can recognize the degrees of suicidal risk (thought, threat, attempt) by the three stages of clinical depression with which they correspond. Expect to hear members of the group speak of their *thoughts* of suicide, and encourage them to bring their thoughts freely into the open. Take seriously any *threats* of suicide, and if the person reports early morning awakening take the necessary precautions to protect his life, to forestall any *attempt* on his part to end it. Of course, any actual attempt will almost automatically result in his being admitted to a hospital. Unless the attempt succeeds. At every point encourage the group members to face their own feelings about all aspects of death, dying, and separation. For, paradoxically, this then becomes preparation for life and living.

IX

Special Concerns:
Homosexuality*

The second concern deserving of special attention before
it comes up in the group is homosexuality. Not that it comes
up as often as suicide. It doesn't. What makes it important
is that when it does come up homosexuality is most likely to
be misunderstood. The therapist needs to keep a clear head
about it if he's to keep others from losing theirs.

Homosexuality has long been one of the tabooed topics
in polite conversation. Not so much any more, fortunately.
People are more open about it now. Still there is much misinformation about homosexuality as well as prejudice based
on that misinformation. Even among professional people
who should know better but honestly don't. Lawyers, judges,
police officers, family physicians, social workers, psychologists,
psychiatrists, all well-intentioned people who must deal with
one aspect or another of homosexuality, find themselves at a
loss.

Unfortunately, we are usually no better off after trying
to read up on the subject. Often we wind up more confused
than ever. The trouble seems to be that what we read about
homosexuality doesn't seem to square with our personal experience with it in either our private or professional lives.

---

*Adapted from an article by the author titled "Homosexuality; a con-
fused trinity" which appeared in *Group Process*, Vol. 6, 1974, pp. 73-82, published by Gordon and Breach Science Publishers Ltd., Great Britain.

You have probably heard the term *homosexual* often applied to an individual as though to describe him or her. When used like this it carries the strong implication that everything of importance that needs to be said about that person has been said, as if the one word conveys all. It doesn't, of course. No one word can. But the unmistakable message is clear: all homosexuals are alike. Know one and you know them all. How simple can we get?

Nevertheless, the notion that homosexuality is the same wherever you find it is quite common. When we hold to this idea and try to apply it across the board we run into numerous contradictions and inconsistencies. Then we are apt to feel frustrated, puzzled, and perhaps a little angry that any firm understanding seems to escape us.

Not until we begin to question whether homosexuality is, in fact, the same wherever it appears does the confusion start to clear.

We discover we are not, apparently, dealing with a single, solitary condition at all. We discover homosexuality about like Caesar discovered ancient Gaul. Remember the opening words of his Commentaries: "Omnia Gallia in tres partes divisa est"—all Gaul is divided into three parts. So it is with homosexuality: all homosexuality is divided into three parts.

The situation is rather like the familiar one in general medicine where the first symptom the physician detects is a fever. The fever alerts him. It indicates something is going on with the patient. The doctor doesn't yet know what that something is because an elevated temperature in itself has little meaning. The patient's true condition cannot be understood or diagnosed on the basis of the fever alone. Yet a long-standing premise in medicine states that the presence of a fever signals a disease within the body. The thing to do then is to search for the disease. Once that is found the physician is immediately in a position to understand both the nature of the disorder and the meaning of the fever. Then he knows how to treat the condition or whether, indeed, there is anything at all he can do about it.

The meaning of homosexuality depends on the personality makeup of the homosexual. When we know something of his general personality we will know what his homosexuality means to him. Knowing what his homosexuality means to him in turn enables us to understand what his homosexuality means to his sexual partner and what that relationship between the two persons must be like. These are certainly important aspects of the whole matter of homosexuality.

The fever analogy is useful up to a point. Let's be careful not to carry it too far. While the presence of a fever always reflects a disease process, homosexual activity does not, in my view, always imply disordered psychological function. Indeed, of the three personality types in which homosexuality appears, only two represent disordered (pathological) functioning. The third (the invert, who is exclusively homosexual) is being increasingly accepted as lying within the normal range of human behavior. Curiously, too, the condition which does represent the severest type of disorder in which homosexuality appears as an important element (homosexual panic) involves no homosexual contact whatever! The individual actually fears homosexual contact and it's the last thing in the world he or she desires. But we're getting ahead of ourselves.

What are the three basic personality configurations in which the symptom of homosexuality appears? They are the invert, to use Havelock Ellis's term; the paranoid personality; and the antisocial personality. The homosexual element embedded within each of these three personality contexts we call essential homosexuality, latent homosexuality, and incidental homosexuality, respectively.*

The invert is the person who is exclusively homosexual, who does not have and does not want sexual relations with the opposite sex. Ellis[1] chose the term *invert* deliberately to avoid the word *pervert* and the activity as perversion. He did so after Freud defined perversions to be all sexual activities among adults except the union of male and female genitals. (Not many would accept this definition nowadays!) Freud[2] further stated that "neurosis is the negative of a perversion." This means, Clara Thompson[3] explains, that "neurotic symptoms represent repression of perverse sexual interests. Perversion, on the other hand, does not spring from repression. In the perversions infantile sexual interests remain conscious and receive gratification. Because there is satisfactory discharge of the libido there is no damming of energy and repression does not take place. This logically brought Freud to the conclusion that in the case of perversions there is no neurosis and nothing can be analyzed."

To the extent that the exclusive homosexual, the invert, is not conflicted about his homosexual orientation and is therefore not neurotic about it, to that extent the statement

---

*We are beginning to hear young adults who describe themselves as bisexual. They seem to mean that they have learned not to discriminate in their loving and therefore in their choice of lovers. Hence at any time the partner can be same sex or opposite sex. To bisexuals love is the important thing, not the sex of the loved one. It is too soon to know whether they actually constitute a fourth category of homosexuality.

[1]Ellis, Havelock. *Studies in the Psychology of Sex.* Vol. 2. 1942. Random House, New York.

[2]Freud, Sigmund. *Three contributions to the theory of sex.* 1930. New York: Nervous and Mental Disease Publishing Co.

[3]Thompson, Clara. *Psychoanalysis: evolution and development.* 1950. New York: Hermitage House.

is true and accurate. However, the exclusively homosexual individual may be conflicted and therefore neurotic in areas of his life having little or nothing to do with his homosexuality. Freud clearly concurred with this point of view when he stated in a letter to an American mother[4] regarding her son's homosexuality: "What analysis can do for your son runs in a different line. If he is unhappy, neurotic, torn by conflicts, inhibited in his social life, analysis may bring him harmony, peace of mind, full efficiency, whether he remains homosexual or gets changed."

It is for these difficulties in other areas of his life that the invert personality may seek and benefit from psychotherapy, at least to the extent that heterosexual patients do. He or she is characteristically content with his or her* homosexual orientation. This is not what bothers him, and he wants that part of himself left alone. Indeed, it may be for the very reason that the invert personality does accept his homosexuality so openly that he is rarely seen in psychiatric outpatient clinics or as admissions to psychiatric wards. Again, when he does appear in these places it is apt to be for reasons other than his homosexuality.

The findings of Dr. Evelyn Hooker's[5] landmark study are well worth noting here. She wished to find out whether homosexuals are as adjusted in their lives as are heterosexuals in theirs. But she avoided the traditional procedure of lumping all "homosexuals" together by carefully selecting

[4]*Sex Information and Education Council of the U.S. (SIECUS) Newsletter.* 1970, 6, 5.

*Hereafter, for ease of presentation I will use the masculine pronoun (he, him, his) only, with the understanding that the reference applies to the female homosexual as well.

[5]Hooker, Evelyn. A preliminary analysis of group behavior of homosexuals. *J. Psychol.,* 1956, 42, 217-225. Hooker, Evelyn. The adjustment of the male overt homosexual. *J. Proj. Tech.,* 1957, 21, 18-31.

for study only those male homosexuals who openly identified themselves as such, whose patterns of sexual desires and overt sexual behavior were predominantly or exclusively directed toward members of their own sex, who were not seeking psychological help, and who were gainfully employed. (It happens that these criteria describe exactly the first of the three personality categories we are delineating here, the one referred to as the invert personality whose homosexuality is essential and exclusive.) Dr. Hooker proceeded to match thirty overt male homosexuals with thirty heterosexuals on the basis of age, education, and intelligence. She then administered a series of projective techniques and attitude scales and gathered further information from intensive life history interviews. All of this material was presented to a panel of experienced clinicians with the request that they rate each subject on a 5-point scale of adjustment. The specific sexual orientation of each of the subjects was, of course, withheld from the judges. The findings were clear and unambiguous: the ratings of adjustment for homosexuals and for heterosexuals were not significantly different. Furthermore, the judges found it impossible to distinguish between the two groups. They were generally unable to pick out the homosexual person in the thirty matched pairs.

What is the personality of the invert like, aside from being well adjusted and being exclusively homosexual? He is apt to be above average in intelligence, with a level of education at a par with his intelligence. He tends to be of a refined nature, preferring the more cultured tastes. Hence he is drawn to the arts though the social sciences and religion attract him too. He is capable of strong devotion and loyalty. It appears that his homosexual affairs and marriages are as stable and enduring as are the affairs and marriages of heterosexual people. He can be just as downcast and despondent over the loss of a homosexual lover as the heterosexual

can be on losing his lover. He is as apt to be prey to feelings
of jealousy as are people who are not homosexual. He is
gregarious, seeking especially the company of other homosexuals, though he also enjoys the company of other persons
of culture and refinement who are able to accept him as
he is. Should psychopathology develop it is likely to be a mild
psychoneurosis not centered primarily around his homosexuality, or a psychosomatic condition. He experiences severe psychological disorder or psychosis only rarely.

By contrast, the homosexuality which appears in the context of the paranoid personality is distinctly different from
essential homosexuality as described above. This kind of
homosexuality is the latent homosexuality of traditional psychiatry. The person with latent homosexuality cannot accept
it in any sense. Any trace of it in himself or even any implication that it might be there becomes a source of constant
threat to him.

Classical psychopathology asserts that embedded within
every paranoid condition lies a homosexual conflict. Experienced clinicians have met with enough exceptions to this
assumption to question its generality. Though homosexual
conflict does occur in many paranoid cases there are many
instances in which no such conflict can be found. To expect
to find it, therefore, in every paranoid disorder is definitely
misleading. The old assumption looks more and more like
a myth or perhaps a half-truth. No useful purpose is served
in continuing it.

But the paranoid personality who does have to contend
with latent homosexuality as part of his makeup lives as
though he were under an ever-present threat. He must remain always alert and on guard against this threat, which he
perceives as coming from either of two directions. One is
from within himself. The other is from without, from the

social environment in which he must live and from the people who surround him.

When the life situation is such that the paranoid personality with latent homosexuality is forced into close and relatively intimate quarters with persons of the same sex the threat intensifies and may become intolerable. The individual passes from mild uneasiness to discomfort to agonized distress until at last he becomes disorganized, he "goes to pieces," and is left in the fearfulness of what is called homosexual panic. The military services are well acquainted with this sequence of events among military personnel. Barracks life with its confinement, where all must share the same bed space, toilet and bathing facilities, is ultimately unendurable for the person with latent homosexuality of this sort.

The paranoid individual with latent homosexuality will go to great lengths to assure himself and others that he is not "tainted" with homosexuality of any sort or in any degree. This effort in fact becomes a central theme in his life. A frequent strategy is to seek marriage with a person of the opposite sex so as to look "normal" in the eyes of the world. The chosen partner is likely to take the marriage in good faith, without the faintest idea that she (or he) is serving a special purpose. She may become aware over time that he has little emotional warmth for her, that he seems to prefer distance to closeness. He may want a child or even children but they, too, are for display purposes only. If his wife approaches him with her dissatisfaction he is apt to insist that he is content with things as they are in the relationship, can see no reason for change, and won't speak of divorce. The underlying reason for his attitude, of course, is that the marriage stands as self-evident proof to himself and to the world that he is fully and entirely heterosexual. The symbolic value of the marriage for him is therefore priceless.

Hence he must keep the marriage intact at all costs. He hangs on to it with desperation. Happiness is not what he is looking for in marriage. What he seeks is simply some measure of relief from the relentless threat of his latent homosexuality.

The third basic personality type associated with homosexual behavior is the antisocial personality. This is the current term for what used to be called the sociopath and, earlier, the psychopath.

The homosexual behavior which occurs in connection with the antisocial personality is almost accidental because it seems to happen more by chance than by deliberate preference. Perhaps incidental describes this type of homosexuality more accurately. A closer look at the general characteristics which define the antisocial (sociopathic) personality will make this clear.

The sociopath does not feel bound by the conventions of society. This places him, therefore, in the basic position of being free to do very much as he pleases. However, since he is not psychotic and does remain in close touch with reality, he keeps a wary eye on the law as he moves along. Because he lacks a conscience he is capable of experiencing little or no primary guilt feelings. However, he is able to experience guilt feelings of a different sort, a kind of secondary guilt. It is what he feels when he gets caught for breaking the law. He berates himself for getting caught, not for acting wrongly. His tolerance for frustration is always low. He cannot endure putting off for long what he wants right away. Whatever it is, he must have it now. His every need must be gratified promptly whether it's for food, drink, money, sleep, sex, or anything else.

When he needs sex any compliant partner will do. For this reason he might as easily be thought of as ambisexual (or bisexual), for it's largely a matter of indifference to the sociopath whether the willing partner happens to be of the same sex or of the opposite sex. Obviously, when his partner turns out to be of the same sex the relationship is homosexual. It could just as easily be the other way around. This is why the adjective *incidental* or *accidental* seems to fit this type of homosexuality. But regardless of the sex of the partner of the moment the relationship is typically short and passing, a one-night stand. The sociopathic personality shows little or no emotional investment in his partner, male or female. He doesn't want to be tied down in any way to anyone. He is also boastful, inclined to brag freely and openly about any of his activities when he feels it safe to do so. He relates his sexual exploits with equal glee and gusto, having little consideration for the feelings or welfare of his partner. And since he rarely hesitates to take full advantage of him these sexual encounters frequently become sadistic and murderous, depending on the impulse of the moment.

The table shown here summarizes the differential features of the homosexuality associated with each of the three personality types. These features stand out most clearly as you read down the columns.

Thus the first column, headed Partner Choice, indicates that the person with Essential Homosexuality will choose a partner of the same sex, while the Latent Homosexual chooses a partner of the opposite sex, and the Incidental Homosexual will accept partners of either sex.

The second column describes the homosexual's emotional attachment to the partner of his choice. Again reading downward, you see that the Essential Homosexual's attachment to his partner is firm and enduring; the attachment of the Latent Homosexual to his partner loose yet enduring; and the attachment of the Incidental Homosexual to his partner superficial, temporary, and changing (or shallow, short, and shifting).

The next column headed Ego Reaction deals with the attitudes of the three categories of homosexual toward conscious awareness of their homosexual inclinations. We see that the ego reaction of the Essential Homosexual is conscious acceptance, that is to say, it is ego-syntonic. By contrast, the Latent Homosexual's ego reaction is conscious rejection, or ego-alien. And for the Incidental Homosexual his ego reaction is conscious acceptance—the sociopath doesn't care who knows about his sexual behavior, really, provided the police are not listening.

With knowledge of the particular ego reaction in each instance one can readily infer whether guilt feeling is present or absent. The next column notes the presence or absence of guilt feelings for each of the three kinds of homosexuality. The Essential Homosexual experiences little or no guilt concerning his homosexuality. By contrast again, the Latent Homosexual is plagued by a strong, almost inescapable sense of guilt. The Incidental Homosexual, on the other hand, displays no guilt about anything in his antisocial life, including his sexuality, homosexual or otherwise.

What is the outcome likely to be if psychological stress develops and intensifies in each of the three homosexual configurations? The last column suggests what may be expected. The Essential Homosexual may develop a mild neurosis or psychosomatic condition, with jealousy and despondency frequently present. The outcome for the Latent Homosexual is homosexual panic and paranoid psychosis. Under stress the Incidental Homosexual simply reinforces his basic antisocial personality to become even more openly sociopathic. Because he will give way more frequently to his violent, hostile, and aggressive impulses he'll have a harder time evading the law. And the frequency of unnatural deaths will be greater for sociopathic homosexuals and their partners than for the other two categories.

HOMOSEXUAL BEHAVIOR ASSOCIATED WITH THREE BASIC PERSONALITY STRUCTURES

BASIC PERSONALITY	*PARTNER CHOICE*	*HOMOSEXUAL BEHAVIOR*			*PATHOLOGICAL OUTCOME*
		PARTNER ATTACHMENT	*EGO REACTION*	*GUILT FEELINGS*	
INVERT (Essential homo.)	Same sex	Firm and enduring	Conscious acceptance	Absent	Mild psychoneurosis (jealousy)
PARANOID (Latent homo.)	Opposite sex	Loose and enduring	Conscious rejection	Present	Homosexual panic and paranoid psychosis
SOCIOPATH (Incidental homo.)	Either sex	Superficial, temporary, and changing	Conscious acceptance	Absent	Antisocial behavior

What I have presented here is a descriptive frame of reference within which three kinds of homosexuality become understandable when seen in the context of one of the basic personality configurations of which they are a part. Nothing is said concerning origins and etiology. That will require further inquiry.

Many years of teaching in a medical school show that this descriptive framework is useful for several reasons. It removes homosexuality as a hazy, shapeless concept and replaces it with three fairly well delineated patterns of attitudes toward persons of the same sex, with each of the three taking meaning from the basic personality types of which they are a part. Our diagnostic conclusions are sounder because they are based on a firmer understanding. And consequently we are in a better position to know what to do about it when confronted with homosexuality in any given instance.

This is important to you when you are leading a therapy group because you carry a large portion of the responsibility for who comes into the group as a patient. When you are considering a person as a group prospect it is not enough to know that there is some element of homosexuality about him (or her). You need to know the nature of the homosexuality and what it means to him in the light of his basic personality. With that information you're able to decide whether to take him into the group.

For example, I will no longer accept a person for group therapy whose homosexuality is of the incidental sort, not because of his homosexuality but because it ties in with his sociopathic personality. If he is a typical sociopath, he is likely to be disruptive in the group, unlikely to develop any sense of belonging or identification, and unlikely to learn any lessons from his experiences in the group. The other group members, including the therapist, may feel endlessly frustrated in their efforts to reach him or to develop any meaningful relationship with him—rather much to his delight. As a result, nobody benefits.

I will also not accept an individual into group psychotherapy who is struggling with latent homosexuality. His constant fear that others might perceive him to be the slightest bit homosexual makes his experience in the therapy group—as in any group—a painful one. His need to be always on guard puts the group on edge, with the feeling that they must be careful what they say or do at all times. Hence the group is blocked from carrying out the therapeutic work it has come together to do. Again, nobody gains.

The situation is quite different with persons who are exclusively, essentially, homosexual. I readily accept such people into therapy groups. Provided they want to come. For I understand, and they realize I understand, that their homosexuality is not at issue. Other things may be bothering them in their relationships with people that have little or nothing to do with their sexuality. In the group they are sensitive to others, in the positive sense, do establish close feeling relationships—with both sexes—do identify with the group, and do share in the responsibility for seeing that the group moves toward its goal.

Here it is important to remember that group members often look to you as the group therapist for cues and leads. In their minds they ask, "What is his (your's, the therapist's) attitude?" They do this most frequently when emergencies come up in group or when the talk turns to death and dying, like suicide. They do it also when homosexuality comes up. They probably carry the full bag of misinformation and prejudice which surrounds that subject. But with one difference: they're ready to learn better. You can give them that opportunity.

X

Who's for What

Group psychotherapy and the small group field can, and do, accommodate many different approaches to the handling of groups. The variations come about as a result of differing theories of personality structure and function, differing notions about the nature of psychotherapy and small group process, and, finally, of differing techniques actually used within groups. This is where things start getting complicated —and confusing. You will be amazed at the number of different approaches you will come across if you stay in this area of interest for any time at all. You will also be impressed by the vigor and richness of all that is happening here. Dynamic, moving, ongoing, alive, are good descriptive words—anything but static, stationary, dull, or boring.

The first section below offers a selected sample of some of the better-known, established approaches that are recognized by professional psychologists, psychiatrists, and clinical social workers. Remember, this whole book is for openers only. It's to give you some idea of what the field is all about and what it's really like. If you care to know more, you'll find where to go for it in Chapter 13.

Since organizations and what they stand for are important, too, the prominent ones will be discussed in the chapter which follows.

APPROACHES AND PEOPLE

Group Psychoanalysis

Or analysis in groups. Not the daddy, but the granddaddy of all the many variations in group therapy today. Most of them, anyway. As mentioned earlier (page 14), this approach carries over into therapy groups the principles, concepts, and techniques of Sigmund Freud's psychoanalysis which he developed for the treatment of individual patients. When you hear of a group that is analytically oriented this tells you the therapist is trying to adhere as closely as possible to traditional Freudian psychoanalytic therapy.

This can't be done exactly, of course. The physical arrangement doesn't permit it. Freud had his patients lie on a couch while he seated himself behind them, out of sight. In this way his presence would be less of a distraction to them as they followed his fundamental rule of free association, which was that they were to put into words every thought, image, sensation, feeling, dream, or anything else that came to mind. This was the royal road to the unconscious. For Freud it was a better way of reaching the unconscious than hypnosis—which he was not very good at.

People in therapy groups sit in a circle with the group therapist facing each other. All are in clear view of each other, no one is hidden from the rest. This change in seating arrangement is an obvious departure from the original. Some psychoanalysts say the difference is so important that what is left cannot be called psychoanalysis. Other psychoanalysts disagree, insisting that the associations touched off in group interaction are an adequate, and even richer, replacement for the old free association, and that as long as transferences, resistances, and dreams receive the primary emphasis in the group experience the result is certainly psychoanalysis.

SAM SLAVSON, father of group psychotherapy in this country and founder of the American Group Psychotherapy Association, is psychoanalytically oriented. He has written several books on group therapy, all of them from the psychoanalytic point of view, including a textbook. ALEXANDER WOLF, a psychiatrist and training analyst, has for many years associated with EMANUEL K. SCHWARTZ, a clinical psychologist, at the Post Graduate Center for Mental Health in New York City. Well-known as teachers, they have collaborated on a book and several articles. S. H. FOULKES, also a psychiatrist and psychoanalyst, represents England's early entry into the field. ASYA L. KADIS was a longtime, well-beloved teaching member on the staff of the Post Graduate Center for Mental Health. Jointly with two other members of that same organization she wrote a useful little handbook which stresses the psychodynamics of group psychotherapy. The second edition of that book includes contributions from two additional authors, MYRON F. WEINER, M.D., and CHARLES WINICK, Ph.D.

Slavson, S. R. *A textbook in analytic group psychotherapy.* New York: International Universities Press, 1964.

Wolf, A., & Schwartz, E. K. *Psychoanalysis in groups.* New York: Grune & Stratton, 1962.

Foulkes, S. H. *Therapeutic group analysis.* New York: International Universities Press, 1965.

Kadis, A. L., Krasner, J. D., Weiner, M. F., Winick, C., & Foulkes, S. H. *A practicum of group psychotherapy.* Hagerstown, Maryland: Harper & Row, Publishers, 2nd edition, 1974.

Transactional Analysis (T.A.)

ERIC BERNE was a practicing psychiatrist in California whose training was solidly psychoanalytic. As a psychotherapist he found that the special vocabulary, the jargon, of psychoanalysis tended to get in the way of therapy. The words are highly technical, and while trained professionals could work with them, patients found the language difficult to deal with. Consequently, there was a relative breakdown in communication between therapist and patient because they were not speaking the same language.

Berne decided to try to do something about this difficulty. He determined to put the language and the concepts of psychoanalysis into words most people in this day and time could understand and use. To say that his efforts have proved enormously successful would seem somewhat of an understatement in light of the popularity T.A. has gained in this country.

First he dealt with the three parts of the personality. Id he translated into Child, ego he translated into Adult, and superego became Parent. Next he recognized that each of these has an ongoing existence within all of us, so he calls them states—the Child state, the Adult state, the Parent state—of a person's being. Then, since most people don't live without contacts with other people who have their own individual Child, Adult, and Parent states, he realized that these relationships can be seen as communications between a given state in one person with a given state in another. For example, one person may be speaking from his Parent state and be heard from the Child state of the person he is talking to. These communications Berne calls transactions. Transactions between two people can be analyzed and diagrammed fairly easily. Hence the term transactional analysis. By now the three circles with a P, A, and C inside are familiar symbols to people from coast to coast.

Two other distinctive aspects of the T.A. approach need to be mentioned. One has to do with decisions, first as children growing up and later as adults. As youngsters we build up images of ourselves from what people, particularly parents, tell us. We figure, as kids, they're in a position to know what they are talking about. So whether we like it or not we buy what they say. Often they don't even have to say what they think, they can get their message over by what they do without saying a word. We don't have to accept their notions about us, of course, though we usually do. Either way, whether we do or we don't, we're making a decision.

Suppose, for example, your mother told you repeatedly years ago that you had no character (whatever that is). In spite of yourself you decided she must be right. You've carried this notion with you over the years, convinced that you have no character. Now, however, you're an adult and you've learned a lot along the way. Now you're in a position to be your own judge, to look at this description of yourself from an adult's point of view, and to decide whether the description really fits or whether to discard it. In T.A. terms this is re-decision. It brings back into the process of psychotherapy a person's freedom to choose. It emphasizes the patient's responsibility for himself and reminds him he can exercise a free will. You don't have to go on being the hapless victim of your childhood.

A second distinctive aspect of the T.A. approach deals with contracts. Therapists with other approaches often accept patients for psychotherapy who are unhappy about their lives, or feel miserable in general, or want to improve themselves. These reasons are not specific enough for a T.A. therapist. He insists that you be very precise on what you are coming for and what you want to work on. That way the goal is clear at the outset. If the therapist agrees to work with you toward that goal, then you have a contract with each other. Since the goal is well defined from the beginning the patient and everybody else, including the therapist, can tell when it is reached. Therapy comes to a successful end. No need for it to go on interminably.

Berne's first book on T.A., *Transactional Analysis in Psychotherapy,* is a serious book for professional readers. His next book, *Games People Play,* turned out to be one of the best sellers of all time. THOMAS A. HARRIS, also a psychiatrist who lives in California, wrote a book titled *I'm OK —You're OK.* It, too, caught on and has added greatly to the popularity of T.A. Although many other books and pamphlets on T.A. are now available, these three remain basic reading.

Berne, E. *Transactional analysis in psychotherapy.* New York: Grove Press, 1961.

Berne, E. *Games people play.* New York: Grove Press, 1964.

Harris, T. A. *I'm OK—You're OK.* New York: Harper & Row, Publishers, 1967.

Gestalt

The word is German and keeps its German pronunciation even in English. That means the *G* is hard, as in *get,* and the *S* has an *ish* sound, as in *dish.* So the word comes out as *gishtalt* with the accent on the second syllable. Roughly it means pattern or configuration.

Gestalt is the name of a school of psychology which has had a powerful impact on both science and modern man. Gestalt therapy is closely related to it.

Gestalt psychology is based on a number of principles, many having far-reaching implications.

A first principle states that the world for any person can only be what that person experiences it to be with his or her own senses. It doesn't really matter what others tell you the world is like; it's only what you perceive for yourself that matters. This point of view is called phenomenology.

It follows from the above viewpoint that for the individual person everything is relative rather than absolute. Relative here means more-or-less, while absolute means either-or. For example, honesty is not an absolute but a relative trait in human nature: the absolute view holds that a person is either honest or he's not honest; the relative view holds that a person is more or less honest, depending on the circumstances. The rich boy who is not a good student may cheat on exams but won't steal, whereas the poor boy who is a good student may steal but won't cheat on exams. Hence honesty is relative.

Another principle of Gestalt psychology states that every person organizes his experience of the world in a way that is meaningful for him. This is perception. The process goes on both consciously and unconsciously. It results in selective attention and selective inattention. Anything new that seems to fit in with our own experience we are inclined to attend to and accept, whereas anything new that does not fit in we are likely to ignore and reject. We see this most clearly when witnesses take the stand to testify and when patients give the history of their illnesses. In most cases when they omit details it's not because they are trying to distort or hide the truth but because those details are not important from their point of view. Memory, of course, is also influenced by the way we perceive things.

Do you remember being taught in school that the whole can never be greater than the sum of its parts? The ancient

Greek mathematicians thought so. They planted the idea as a basic assumption for all of science, and the idea has been passed along from generation to generation to the present. Until Gestalt psychology came along. The Gestaltists questioned this long-standing assumption and found it is not always true. The whole can be, and often is, greater than the sum of its parts.

After the Gestaltists proved this to be the case people began to find further examples everywhere. For instance, when we transpose a line of music we still easily recognize the melody even though the actual physical sound stimulus is entirely different. In the field of medicine we know we can build up the body from its smallest elements to its highest components, proceeding from biochemistry to cells to tissues to organs to systems, which is about as high as medical science can go. Yet when we put all these parts together do we have a whole man? Is that all there is? No, there is something more to man than the sum total of his parts.

The discovery of the new principle that the whole can be greater than the sum of its parts freed the minds of men from the mind-lock of the past. The field of physics, which had gone about as far as it could go while bound to the old assumption, had slowed down almost to a stop. A new world, a whole new universe, opened up. The new knowledge tied in with Einstein's theory of relativity to create deeper understanding. Now man could get to the moon and reach for the stars. Certainly this one contribution alone from Gestalt psychology has had a profound effect on all of us, one which we're just beginning to realize.

Gestalt studies in perception show that when we look around us we see things either as ground or figure. Ground is short for background and figure is the part that stands out, on which we are focusing our attention. For example, as you look at a chalk board which has some writing on it, when you read the writing the writing is figure and the green background is ground. But you can shift the focus of your attention to the green ground, and when you do the green ground becomes figure and the writing recedes into ground. Figure and ground possess this characteristic of being reversible in human awareness. Consciousness is like this, too. Thoughts, sensations, feelings, and so forth, can emerge from the ground of unawareness (the unconscious) to become figures as we become fully aware of them. However, only one thing can be in the forefront of consciousness at any one time. Something else will take its place when it moves back into ground, and that something else takes its turn being figure.

One important study in Gestalt psychology demonstrates that tasks which are not completed are more easily and vividly remembered than tasks which are fully completed. This is known as the Zeigarnik effect. Gestalt psychotherapy applies this knowledge in a practical way when it refers to unfinished business in a patient's life. That unfinished business has to be finished in the present before it can be put away once and for all.

Mention of Gestalt therapy always calls to mind the name of FREDERICK S. ("FRITZ") PERLS, M.D., Ph.D., who originated this form of psychotherapy. Though Perls had sound training as a psychoanalyst, he was dissatisfied with certain aspects of psychoanalysis as a way of treating patients. Perhaps what bothered him most was that it is too slow, takes too long with each patient, and therefore makes it impossible for one therapist to see more than a handful of patients in individual therapy over a period of time. The Gestalt therapy he developed loses no time with any person who wants to work in therapy—and he wasted no time on anybody who wasn't ready to work.

Gestalt therapy focuses exclusively on the present, on what is happening here and now in a person's experience.

Even the past is unimportant except as something still happening in the present. The future doesn't count, either, because it is not here yet and therefore doesn't really exist. The Gestaltists make a big point of this business of staying in the present.

Anxiety is conceived as a kind of stage fright that comes about as one thinks of the future and begins rehearsing for it in one's mind. The remedy for anxiety, therefore, is to return from the future to give one's attention to the present. When you become intensely aware of the present then anxiety disappears.

Focusing entirely on one's present experience and becoming fully aware of it does not come about as easily and readily as one might suppose. It takes practice. To this end Perls devised a number of exercises to develop what he terms an awareness continuum.

Perls is also insistent that every person take full responsibility for himself and his actions. He points out how in our everyday speech we use language to avoid personal responsibility. "*It* made me mad" is nonsense; we mean, "I got mad." The use of "you" in a general, impersonal sense when we really mean "I" or "me" is another example. "You get angry and hurt when he treats you like that" really means "I get angry and hurt. . . ." We become more of a whole person when we speak directly with full responsibility for what we experience.

For Freud dreams always represented some sort of wish-fulfillment. Not so with Perls, who took dreams to be existential messages from the dreamer to himself (the dreamer). Dreams consistently center about holes in the personality of the dreamer. Gestalt therapists devote considerable time to working on a patient's dreams, finding that this does much to further self-understanding.

Perls had a way of saying things directly and concisely.

He didn't waste words. He wasn't afraid of them, either. For instance, he liked to point to three classes of superficial communication among persons which he calls chickenshit, bullshit, and elephantshit. When you read Perls you'll find him alive, vigorous, and compelling. He does practice what he preaches.

The Gestalt Prayer, which Perls wrote, has become widely known:

> I do my thing, and you do your thing.
> I am not in this world to live up to your expectations.
> And you are not in this world to live up to mine.
> You are you and I am I,
> And if by chance we find each other, it's beautiful.
> If not, it can't be helped.

Perls, F. S. *The Gestalt Approach & Eyewitness to Therapy*. Ben Lomond, California: Science & Behavior Books, 1973.

Perls, F. S. *Gestalt therapy verbatim*. Lafayette, California: Real People Press, 1969.

Perls, F. S. *In and out the garbage pail*. Lafayette, California: Real People Press, 1969.

Psychodrama

As the name suggests, psychodrama provides a patient with a means for expressing himself and his personal hangups through spontaneous action within the therapy group session. Thus it represents rather more of a technique in therapy than a unique and different way of understanding human nature and human relations.

JACOB L. MORENO, M.D., the father of psychodrama and sociometry, made his headquarters at Beacon, New York, where he established the Moreno Institute. He was impressed by the emotional release (catharsis) afforded both actors and audience by the ancient Greek dramas. Moreno states he simply picked up where they left off. He and his wife, ZERKA MORENO, have brought his ideas along to the point where psychodrama now holds a lasting place in group psychotherapy and the small group field.

The simplest form of psychodrama consists of role-playing. It can be used easily in regular therapy groups. Usually a patient plays himself in a particular situation involving another person, say his mother, with some person in the group playing the role of mother. Suppose the patient has been wanting to tell his mother of his plan to get married but hasn't been able to face her with it. The therapist might ask some willing woman in the group to play the patient's mother. Then the patient is instructed to talk with her as though she were his mother, and she responds as though she were. This kind of rehearsal often frees a patient to carry out what he needs to do in real life.

The more elaborate form of psychodrama requires a stage and a cast of characters. Yes, quite literally, a stage and a cast of characters as well as an audience. The therapist becomes the director of a play which he produces. The play, of course, involves the patient's life and is intended as an opportunity for the patient to bring his private world into the open where it can be faced and dealt with.

Moreno thinks of the procedure as using five instruments. The stage is one. It symbolizes the stage of life, providing the patient with an actual life space within which he is free to move. The patient or subject, too, is an instrument, a rather obvious one. So is the therapist or director, who also interprets or analyses what goes on as is appropriate. The fourth instrument consists of the therapeutic aides, also called auxiliary egos, who play the persons in the patient's life drama. The last instrument, surprisingly, is the audience, but this is no ordinary audience. It is expected to react to what it sees and hears on stage and to do so openly, not passively or silently. This is a lively audience, indeed. It far outdoes the typical audience reaction to the good old-fashioned melodramas we're all familiar with.

This kind of psychodrama gets to be pretty technical. Any group therapist who plans to make use of it needs to obtain special training in the method. It requires considerable activity on the part of the therapist, more than many therapists are able to tolerate or maintain.

Moreno, J. L. *Psychodrama,* Vol. 1. Beacon, New York: Beacon House, 1946.

Moreno, J. L. & Moreno, Z. T. *Psychodrama,* Vol. 2. Beacon, New York: Beacon House, 1952.

Moreno, J. L. *Psychodrama and group psychotherapy.* 3rd Ed. New York: Beacon House, 1957.

Encounter Groups

CARL R. ROGERS. A name widely known and respected. One of the outstanding psychologists of our time. He has made numerous contributions as a clinician, as a scientific investigator, and as a teacher. Among the many things for which he will be remembered is the fact that he opened therapeutic interviews to scientific study by being the first to record what actually takes place in them, using the new invention of the wire recorder to do so.

During the early period of his professional career Dr. Rogers developed an approach to therapeutic interviewing which he called non-directive. It aroused considerable interest and gained many adherents among psychologists, psychiatrists, social workers, and others who took the time to understand it. Because it was new and competed with the older approaches Rogerian non-directive counseling and therapy could not help becoming controversial as well. It was described in caricature by some as creating a vacuum in the direction you wanted the patient to move.

When Rogers realized that the term non-directive did lend itself a little too easily to being misconstrued he coined the term *client-centered* to replace it. The new term does succeed in conveying the essence of Rogers's approach, which is to focus on the person being interviewed from the point of view of that person rather than from the point of view of the interviewer. Client-centered also makes it clear that the approach is no longer limited to patients as such. Still it can be misunderstood. People who have only a little knowledge of client-centered therapy describe it as parroting back the patient's or client's words just as he said them—again, a caricature of what Rogers intends.

Rogers's approach rests on attitude, not technique. The attitude can be implemented and taught, and this in itself is a major achievement. Anyone who takes client-centered therapy to be nothing more than a technique is sadly mistaken and has missed the point completely.

The therapist who uses the client-centered approach attempts to gain an understanding of the patient by listening closely to the patient's feelings and attitudes. Feelings, mind you, not the words. "*I* love you," "I *love* you," and "I love *you?*" all have different meanings and express different feelings even though the words are the same in each case. The therapist will rephrase what he believes he hears the person saying, and he'll put the rephrasing as a question to find out how close his understanding is to what the person intends. The therapist, on hearing the first of the above phrases reported by a patient in an exchange with his (the patient's) son, might respond to the patient, "*You* love your son, although there may be others in the family you feel may not love him, is that it?" The patient can say, "Yes, that's so." Or he can say, "No, that's not quite what I mean," and go on to clarify. In doing so, of course, he comes to a clearer understanding of what he himself really feels. In any case, the patient in this way is always in a position to let the therapist know if he, the therapist, is on target. As you see, the questions used in client-centered therapy are neither probing, intrusive, nor interpretive.

In his early years Rogers was very much of a clinician. The business of a clinician, of course, is disease. He studies disease to recover health. Nevertheless, the disease orientation began to bother Rogers. Perhaps he is by nature too humane, too optimistic about human beings to have been content to go through life seeing people at their worst, people diseased. He is inclined toward a positive view of life, a humanist with a deep faith in persons. Little wonder that he slowly moved away from the relatively cold, impersonal, objective world of the clinician.

And where did he move? He moved into groups. Here he could have people by the dozens. They could have him, and they could have each other. He wants to put people in touch with one another and in touch with themselves. These contacts when they occur are encounters. Encounters lead to personal growth. Putting together all the encounters now taking place and likely to take place as the movement sweeps the country amounts to a social revolution.

Rogers has come to avoid the term *therapist* for himself, nor does he consider what he presently accomplishes with groups to be psychotherapy. Rogers is struck by the fact that the encounter group movement has grown up outside of, and in spite of, the "establishment" of academic psychology and psychiatry. It may be, therefore, that a large part of his reason for shunning the words *therapy* and *therapist* is that they are "establishment" words. So instead he describes himself as a facilitator whose function is to facilitate authentic interaction among and between persons. He succeeds beautifully. And it's worth noting that his basic approach to persons has not altered in any important respect from that which he had developed earlier

Rogers, C. R. *Client-centered therapy.* Boston: Houghton Mifflin, 1951.

Rogers, C. R. *Carl Rogers on encounter groups.* New York: Harper & Row, 1970

Existentialism

The word is a mouthful, and you may get the impression you're getting into something deep, maybe over your head. You may even begin to feel your fears are justified when you discover the many European names associated with existentialism and come across the German words that form part of its language. But don't give up. It's worth knowing about.

The foremost spokesmen for the existential approach in America are ROLLO MAY and HUGH MULLAN. If you want the background and philosophy of existentialism, read May. Although he writes well, the subject makes for heavy reading. Mullan, on the other hand, writes as one practicing psychotherapist to another.

Mullan is a physician and a psychiatrist. He, too, received

thorough training in classical psychoanalysis. Then he became interested in group therapy. At about the same time
he began blending psychoanalysis with a somewhat new emphasis which he first called experiential, then subjective, and
finally existential as he acknowledged his kinship to that
school. His book on group psychotherapy, written in collab-
oration with Max Rosenbaum, a clinical psychologist also
trained in psychoanalysis, reflects the blend of the old and
the new.

Existential psychotherapy introduces an awareness of the
human condition into the therapeutic relationship. Not just
an awareness of the human condition of the patient but an
awareness of the human condition of the therapist as well.
This mutual awareness is important. Existentialism is defined as one's individual quest to find meaning in life while
at the same time one becomes aware of his human condition,
experiences and accepts it. The definition of psychotherapy
follows naturally: it is the shared existence of therapist and
patient (s) .

This idea of shared existence is very real for Mullan. The
hour or hour and a half that he spends with a patient is part
of his life time and part of the patient's life time. They are
in therapy together and they are in life together. Together
they must make their lives count, must find meaning together. One can't change without the other; they change
together or not at all.

You can see that this generates a special kind of intimacy.
It cuts through a lot of the pretense and phoniness in human
relations, the relationship in psychotherapy being no exception. It moves people who experience it.

Mullan allows nothing to stand in the way of this relationship. Forms of address and titles are obstacles because
they force us into social roles. Anyone addressed as "Rev-
erend" must act like a minister and be treated as a minister.

A "Mrs." is one thing, a "Miss" is something else. Likewise, as long as you are a "Dr." the person you are seeing professionally must remain a "patient" and both of you act accordingly. Since "patients" are supposed to be sick people they may go on doing what is expected of them as long as they remain patients, that is, being sick. Therefore Mullan puts titles out of the way and becomes simply Hugh to the person who comes to him for professional services. That person has a first name, too, which Mullan uses. The elimination of titles he calls status denial, and it goes both ways.

This manner of dealing with titles stands in contrast with the psychoanalytic view. In psychoanalytic therapy it doesn't matter what titles are used. What does matter is the patient's need to use them. His choice of "Dr. Mullan" rather than "Hugh" would become something to analyze. What lies behind the choice? That's all that matters.

Of distinct value to therapists regardless of their particular orientation is Mullan's way of looking at emergencies and crises. He sees an emergency as an unexpected opportunity for a person to emerge from a situation either stronger and healthier or weaker and sicker. The person has this choice. He also has the responsibility to make it. The presence of the therapist helps him to maintain his perspective and provides support in the knowledge that he is not alone.

Existential psychotherapy is like Gestalt therapy and Rogers's client-centered therapy in two major respects. All three hold the phenomenological point of view (the real world for any person can only be what he or she perceives it to be, not what others say it is), and all concentrate exclusively on the present, the here-and-now.

May, R. (Ed.) *Existential psychology*. New York: Random House, 1961.

Mullan, H. & Rosenbaum, M. *Group psychotherapy.* New York: Free Press of Glencoe, 1962.

Mullan, H. The psychotherapist is challenged by existentialism. *Pilgrimage,* 1974, 3, 1-10.

Marathon

GEORGE R. BACH must be recognized not only as one of the pioneers in group therapy but also as one of the most forceful, creative, and productive psychotherapists of our time. His 1954 book *Intensive Group Psychotherapy* is still worth reading. He has gone on to innovative work with married couples in therapy, training in constructive aggression, and teaching people how to pair. He originated marathon group therapy, too.

Up to the time he tried the marathon the standard procedure among group therapists in this country was to have their groups meet once a week. The few groups that met two or three times a week were relatively rare exceptions. Occasionally organized groups of therapists met on weekends three or four times a year for workshops or retreats. But not until Bach tried it was there any deliberate attempt to bring patients together for a therapeutic experience lasting a continuous 30 to 40 hours. It turned out to be very intensive and quite successful. Marathons now are a common occurrence.

A typical marathon therapy group consists of twelve to sixteen persons, including both men and women, meeting with one or two therapists. They come prepared to stay together and to eat together. People dress comfortably and casually, so they can sit on the floor. Since cushions are provided they can also stretch out and go to sleep, although some marathons do allow short designated rest periods for all. Persons are usually permitted to leave the group only to use the toilet and for no other reason.

Having the same patients together continuously for this length of time offers the therapist (s) an opportunity to employ a variety of techniques in the interests of the patient. Except for his own preferences or limitations of training the therapist is in no way restricted.

The marathon is, however, wearing on everyone, as you can imagine. The therapist becomes wearied, too, which is one good reason to have two therapists present. Yet this very feature of increasing weariness becomes an advantage rather than a disadvantage in the marathon. After an hour or two, as people grow tired, their defenses begin to drop. As they let down their defenses they become more open, more spontaneous, and less phony. They reveal themselves to each other more readily. Here is the raw material for psychotherapy.

The marathon group seems to hold particular promise for work with adolescents. Teen-agers are usually busily involved in school and social activities which often interfere in their attendance with groups set up in the regular manner to meet for an hour and a half once a week. The frequent absence of one or more members of a group does more than simply interrupt the therapeutic work the group is doing. It is demoralizing as well, and tends to encourage others to do likewise by not taking the group seriously. These difficulties are overcome by the weekend marathon. Much work can be accomplished in a relatively short time and then the teen-agers are freed to go.

ELIZABETH E. MINTZ, Ph.D., has written a beautiful little book on marathon groups. A clinical psychologist trained in psychoanalysis, Dr. Mintz has had extensive experience with this type of group. Her book is a rich gold mine of clinical knowledge. You will gain more from it than just an understanding of what the marathon is like.

Bach, G. R. The marathon group: Intensive practice of intimate interaction. *Psychological Reports,* 1966, 18, 995-1005.

Bach, G. R. Marathon group dynamics. *Psychological Reports,* 1967, 20, 1147-1158.

Mintz, E. E. *Marathon groups: reality and symbol.* New York: Appleton-Century-Crofts, 1971.

Family Therapy

If you've gained the impression that group therapy tends to be relatively vague and lacking in structure, wait till you get to family therapy. Group therapy is well defined, indeed, compared to family therapy.

We're not even sure that what is called family therapy is therapy at all. At least not in the usual technical sense. Sure, we are dealing with people and our intent is to improve their lives. Restaurant operators and home building contractors can say the same thing, yet they are not psychotherapists.

When we think of therapy, or treatment, we generally think of it in relation to some diagnosis, which comes first. Okay. But how do you diagnose a family? If family therapy is really therapy, isn't this part of what we would have to do? Still, nobody seems to have yet figured out a generally acceptable way to diagnose families.

Just the same, family therapy is a convenient handle to use for what we do with a family even if it doesn't meet the strict definition of therapy. Family therapists intend to heal the ailing family and make it well, which is the important thing. And if they succeed in doing this by opening up communication within the family system, as some maintain, instead of doing psychotherapy, what difference does it make? Perhaps family therapy belongs in the small group field rather than in group psychotherapy, and should be so considered.

If there is any question whether family therapy is therapy, there is no question that family is a group. A small group at that. It does fit neatly into the small group field.

When you begin to read up on family therapy and observe family therapists in action you are likely to get the idea everybody is out doing his or her own thing. And you'd be pretty near right. You would have good cause to be somewhat bewildered.

Although there isn't much agreement on any aspect of family therapy, three people have achieved outstanding prominence in the field. One is a social worker—and a woman; one is a psychiatrist; and one is a clinical psychologist. They present three different points of view, each quite plausible and sound. Reading them is like becoming acquainted with three faces of truth.

The social worker is VIRGINIA SATIR, a dynamic personality who continues to influence not only the families she works with in therapy but also the many students and professional people who have contact with her. Her book is a good starting point for reading in this field. NATHAN W. ACKERMAN is the psychiatrist whose writing represents the more traditional psychoanalytic, psychodynamic view of family treatment. Nevertheless, he describes himself as being a humanist rather than a mechanist in his approach to troubled families. GERALD H. ZUK, the clinical psychologist, sets out by recognizing that if family therapists have anything at all in common it is that they all are highly active in their sessions with families. He then goes on to describe his function in the family session as being twofold: first he is a go-between; then he takes sides, openly and deliberately. He further recognizes that if individual therapy is a two-way (dyadic) process between therapist and patient then family therapy must be a three-way (triadic) process involving the therapist and any two members of a family at a time. The therapist always establishes himself as a significant force in the interaction among family members.

Satir, V. *Conjoint family therapy*. Palo Alto, Calif.: Science & Behavior Books, 1964.

Ackerman, N. W. *Treating the troubled family*. New York: Basic Books, 1966.

Zuk, G. H. *Family therapy: a triadic-based approach*. New York: Behavioral Publications, 1971.

XI

Organizations:
What They Stand for
and Where to Find Them

Any field of human endeavor is known by the organizations it generates. These organizations in turn produce publications designed either to spread knowledge and know-how or to keep members in touch with each other and the parent organization, or both. Here are the major ones in group therapy and the small group field, arranged alphabetically.

American Academy of Psychotherapists (AAP)

This organization properly belongs at the head of any listing of psychotherapists, even if the accident of alphabetical order didn't place it there. It represents the elite among therapists, including both individual and group psychotherapists. Standards for membership have been set so that virtually all members will primarily be experienced, practiced therapists. Moreover, they've all had personal therapy for themselves, so they not only do it, they've had it. Membership is open to highly qualified psychiatrists, psychologists, social workers, pastoral counselors, and other professional therapists who meet the requirements.

Don't get the idea it's a stuffy outfit. It isn't. The founders of the Academy were frankly tired of abstract, dogmatic, or theoretical papers and meetings. They wanted a true home where they could get together for down-to-earth discussions and demonstrations of therapeutic methods with other practicing therapists. They wanted to know what other therapists actually do in their own offices, not merely what they say they do. The Academy is a vibrant, vigorous, alive organization that cherishes a sense of humor. Its journal, *Voices: The Art and Science of Psychotherapy,* is a beautiful reflection of all that the Academy stands for. The AAP also collects and distributes a *Library of Tape Recordings* of actual sessions with therapists of widely differing orientations, which happens to make a useful learning and teaching aid.

The Academy now has a central office where you can write for membership applications, obtain a Tape Library Catalog, or enter a subscription to *Voices.*

Address: Thomas O. Robinson, Admin. Sec.
American Academy of Psychotherapists
1040 Woodcock Road
Orlando, Florida 32803

American Group Psychotherapy Association (AGPA)

The gathering place for group therapists of all persuasions and therefore the largest organization of its kind in this country. Whereas you must show specific training in Transactional Analysis to become eligible for membership in the International Transactional Analysis Association, even though you are well trained in psychoanalysis or Gestalt therapy, you qualify for membership in the AGPA if you are trained in one of these approaches or in any other recognized method of psychotherapy with groups. AGPA welcomes all. Further, it is willing to listen to new ideas and ways of dealing with groups.

AGPA was founded in 1943 during the years of World War II on the initiative of SAM R. SLAVSON. Slavson, who was associated with the Jewish Board of Guardians in New York City and worked primarily with children and adolescents, was oriented around psychoanalysis. AGPA survived those early years because of his untiring efforts. In turn, his influence was keenly felt and appreciated.

The organization has grown in many ways. You get a real feeling for it as well as its size when you attend one of AGPA's annual meetings. The program offers a wide variety of things to choose from—symposia, workshops, paper-reading sessions, demonstrations, and so on. A regular feast or smorgasbord. In addition, each annual Conference is immediately preceded by a two-day Institute that gives you the opportunity for a small group experience under the leadership of a senior therapist and co-therapist. You don't have to be a member of AGPA to attend either the Conference or the Institute, though you do have to be working with groups professionally.

AGPA has grown geographically, too. Its organizational structure includes regional affiliate societies and local societies within the regions. You are bound to be within reach of one or the other of these—unless you live in Alaska or Hawaii.

The official journal of the AGPA is called the *International Journal of Group Psychotherapy*.

Address: American Group Psychotherapy Association, Inc.
1865 Broadway, 12th Floor
New York, New York 10023

American Society of Group Psychotherapy and Psychodrama (ASGPP)

Not to be confused with the AGPA (above). This is JACOB L. MORENO's organization, which he founded and controlled almost until the time of his death. His wife, ZERKA MORENO, carries on the tradition and the enterprise. The name of the official journal of this organization is *Group Psychotherapy and Psychodrama.*

The distinctive features of Moreno's approach are role playing, psychodrama, and sociometry. Teaching and training in these and related subjects are offered at the Moreno Institute. Students qualify for recognition at four advanced levels designated Auxiliary Ego, Assistant Director, Associate Director, and Director, in that order.

Beacon, New York, has become famous as the headquarters of the many Moreno teaching and publishing activities. Indeed, the Moreno press is named Beacon House, Inc.

Addresses: Moreno Institute, Inc.
              259 Wolcott Avenue
              Beacon, New York 12508

              Beacon House, Inc., Publishers
              P. O. Box 311
              Beacon, New York 12508

Esalen

Esalen is the brainchild of one man, Michael Murphy, who wanted "to bring together a wide variety of approaches toward the enhancement of the human potential" (Esalen Newsletter, 1968). He chose to do this on property he owned at Big Sur, California, which was once the home of an American Indian tribe known as Esalen. Hence Esalen is both a place and an idea, though it may be more accurate to say places because Esalen also has a base now in San Francisco.

Murphy succeeded in transforming his idea into actuality. Esalen did become the home of what is known as the human potential movement and the model for the many growth centers that have sprung up across the country. For this reason its description of itself is worth noting: "Esalen Institute is a center to explore those trends in education, religion, philosophy and the physical and behavioral sciences which emphasize the potentialities and values of human existence. Our activities consist of seminars and workshops, residential programs, consulting and research. . . . We exist to sponsor, encourage, synthesize and attempt evaluation of work in these areas, both inside and outside our own organizational framework. Since we are a center for experimental education, we ask that persons come to our programs out of an educational interest. We ask that no one come whose interest is 'cure.' We point out here, as we have in workshops and seminars, that some persons, particularly those with a history of psychiatric problems, may find some programs difficult, trying, or potentially risky. We recommend that in case of any doubt, a physician or trusted counselor be consulted."

The Esalen Catalog of programs and events gives you some feeling for the climate and spirit of Esalen. It presents an amazing assortment of opportunities for new experiences. Here are some names and terms picked at random from the Catalog: transpersonal, Aikido, Alexander technique, bioenergetic analysis, Feldenkrais exercises, massage, polarity therapy, psychosynthesis, Rolfing, structural integration, T'ai Chi Chuan, Utran, acupuncture, centering, Sufi stories, biofeedback, Wu Chi. How many of these sound familiar to you? Doesn't the list stir your curiosity? When I read it I get the feeling there are a lot of interesting things going on

I know nothing about—but would like to know.

Several people who have used the special atmosphere and facilities of Esalen to develop their own innovative ideas and methods have become well known. Among these are Fritz Perls with his Gestalt therapy, William Schutz and his encounter games, Bernard Gunther with his sensory awareness work, Virginia Satir with her family therapy, and Ida Rolf with her structural integration.

Michael Murphy succeeded so well with Esalen that it is now looked upon as a kind of Mecca by psychotherapists who are not content to go on doing the same old thing in the same old way. They make the pilgrimage and come away feeling satisfied and refreshed in mind and body. Perhaps that's because they, too, are human, and Esalen helped them increase their own potentials.

Take a look at the Esalen Catalog. It's fascinating reading in itself. It comes out quarterly and you can subscribe to it for one year for $2.00. Subscriptions are accepted through the San Francisco office only.

Addresses: Esalen Institute
              Big Sur, California 93920

              Esalen Institute
              1793 Union Street
              San Francisco, California 94123

Growth Centers

Out-growths (!) of the Esalen idea. Independent organizations set up with the same general purpose as Esalen in mind, though on a much smaller scale. You'll find them in large cities all over the U.S.A. by now. The Association for Humanistic Psychology can supply you with a partial listing.

Address: Association for Humanistic Psychology
          325 Ninth Street
          San Francisco, California 94103

International Transactional Analysis Association (ITAA)

Since Eric Berne's *Games People Play* and Thomas Harris's *I'm OK—You're OK* landed on the best-seller list transactional analysis has swept, and is sweeping, the country. Most everybody seems to know something about it. TA terms are becoming part of the language. We hear people say, "Let your Child out." And, "Different strokes for different folks" has become a familiar retort. Classes in TA are springing up all over the land. The International Transactional Analysis Association is the organization that puts it all together—and tries to hold it there.

ITAA is "an educational institute for people in the broad field of social psychiatry." This doesn't mean you have to be a psychiatrist to belong. When ITAA says broad it means broad. Social workers, psychologists, teachers, parole officers and others can all qualify for membership. You may become a Regular Member after taking an Official Introductory Course (called a 101 course). Then, as your training increases, you can move on up the ladder to Clinical Member, Provisional Teaching Member, and finally to Teaching Member.

ITAA issues its own publication, titled the *Transactional Analysis Journal.*

Although you can now obtain training in transactional analysis in almost any part of the United States, the most prominent teaching centers are located in California where TA originated. One of these is the Harris Institute of TA in Sacramento (the Thomas Harris of *I'm OK—You're OK*).

Another popular center that has attracted many people in recent years is one operated by Bob and Mary Goulding (husband and wife), the Western Institute for Group and Family Therapy. Robert L. Goulding, a physician, and Mary L. Goulding, a clinical social worker, are two sparkling, highly enthusiastic, unforgettable personalities.

Addresses: International Transactional Analysis Association
                1722 Vallejo Street
                San Francisco, California 94123

                Transactional Analysis Journal
                3155 College Avenue
                Berkeley, California 94705

                Harris Institute of Transactional Analysis
                2222 Sierra Boulevard
                Sacramento, California 95828

                Western Institute for Group and Family Therapy
                262 Gaffey Road
                Watsonville, California 95076

National Training Laboratories (NTL) Institute for Applied Behavior Science

Yes, it's a mouthful. The name almost weighs it down. No wonder people try to shorten it to something manageable, like NTL Institute. True to its name, it is in fact a vast organization with centers for the experiential laboratory method of learning located on every continent on earth!

Once again, do not let the word laboratory throw you.

When you see laboratory think of group and you'll be safe. In other words, people learn (by experience) interpersonal skills in a group setting, with the emphasis on learn. Participants study their own behavior. This is education, not therapy.

You've heard and read of sensitivity training groups or T-groups (T for training). The NTL Institute is the home of the T-group. The Institute is the organization that grew up around and out of the discovery of the Basic Skills Training Group in Bethel, Maine, back in the summer of 1947. With the T-group as a starter, the NTL Institute has expanded to include group dynamics, organizational development, community development, and, more recently, the development of individual potential in personal growth programs. In this last respect it overlaps or merges with growth centers.

The NTL Institute is organized into three divisions. One, the Programs and Laboratories Division, deals with the programs and events which are open to the general public. The Professional Development Division handles everything related to training people who intend to use the T-group theory and method professionally. It trains trainers or change agents, as T-group leaders are sometimes called. The Contracts and Consultation Division develops special programs for a wide variety of clients and client organizations.

Official publication of the NTL Institute is the *Journal of Applied Behavioral Science.*

Address, for all purposes:

NTL Institute
Box 9155, Rosslyn Station
Arlington, Virginia 22209

Postgraduate Center for Mental Health

Located in New York City, this is one of the most re-
nowned and respected of the centers for the training of
mental health professionals on the East Coast. This is the
place to go if you are looking for the psychoanalytic approach, particularly in group therapy.

Address: Postgraduate Center for Mental Health
           124 East 28th Street
           New York, New York 10016

Synanon

Synanon is almost in a class by itself for several reasons.
First, it succeeds in working with drug addicts when most
others fail. Second, it employs unconventional methods to
achieve its ends. Third, it is run by former addicts for
addicts. Fourth, it has no need for professional psychotherapists.

Drug addiction is one of the most difficult of all human
conditions in the world to treat. Drug addicts just don't usually respond to efforts to help them stay off drugs even after
they have managed to get off drugs for a brief time. Psychotherapy in the usual sense seems to have little or no effect.
Hence any approach that seems to work, as Synanon does,
deserves credit and recognition.

The name Synanon sounds like it must come from the
Greek or Latin and have a hidden meaning. It's nothing of
the sort. It came about as an accident when a newly arrived
addict tripped over his own tongue trying to say symposium
and seminar at the same time. What came out was "syn-

anon." We don't know whether anybody laughed, but the word stuck.

Synanon is a residential center for addicts who wish to cure themselves. They come because they want to, nobody forces them. They live in the Synanon House with other addicts, becoming part of a close community. Importantly, they at the same time submit themselves to the Synanon discipline and treatment.

Synanon is the personal achievement of one man, Charles E. ("Chuck") Dederich, a layman and a long-time alcoholic. With the help of Alcoholics Anonymous he had stopped drinking when in 1958 he started to meet once a week in his apartment with some friends from A.A. for open discussions. He recalls, "The meetings were loud and boisterous. Attack on one another was a keynote of the sessions, with everyone joining in. . . . We would let the air out of pompously inflated egos, including my own. The sessions soon became the high point in everybody's week."

Thus was born Synanon's verbal-attack therapy. It is hard-hitting, often brutal, always direct, and allows no escape or self-deception—and it gets through to the addict where other approaches merely slide off his back, leaving him untouched and unchanged. This is group treatment all right, taken quite literally, treatment *by* the group.

Synanon as an organization has had its difficulties. Yet it has managed to survive and grow. Yablonsky's book tells the story with love and admiration. (Yablonsky, L. *The Tunnel Back: Synanon.* New York: Macmillan, 1965.)

Address: Synanon Foundation, Inc.
6055 Marshall-Petaluma Road
P.O. Box 786
Marshall, California 94940

Tavistock

An English import. The full name is the Centre for Applied Social Research of the Tavistock Institute of London. The Washington School of Psychiatry (located in Washington, D.C., and founded by Harry Stack Sullivan, who developed the principles and therapeutic technique of interpersonal relations) became interested in the Tavistock concept of group relations. The Washington School, convinced that the Tavistock approach would make a useful contribution to the American scene, arranged to bring members of the Tavistock staff to this country to engage in a joint undertaking. The first such conference was held in 1965 at Mount Holyoke College and continues on an annual basis, since 1969, as the A. K. Rice Institute, a branch of the Washington School of Psychiatry. (Rioch, M. J. Group relations: rationale and technique. *International Journal of Group Psychotherapy*, 1970, 22, 340-355.)

Group relations means the relations of one group to another group, not the relation of an individual to a group. However, since groups are made up of individuals the individual cannot be completely ignored. But the primary emphasis lies with the group as a whole as it relates to other groups.

Any society is composed of groups; the more complex the society, the more groups there are. You will find all kinds of groups in this country—political groups, national groups, racial groups, religious groups are some that come quickly to mind. Others are not quite so obvious, like the ones within institutions, large businesses, and industries. Take a hospital, for example. Nurses are a group, and within this group are smaller groups: the registered nurse group, the licensed practical nurse group, the nurses aide group, the ward clerk group. The physicians group likewise contains an intern group, a residents group, a full-time staff group, a visiting staff group. Of course, each department constitutes a group, too, like the Department of Medicine, Department of Surgery, Department of Pediatrics, and so on. Patients form a group, or groups, as well. Housekeeping personnel form a group, physical plant forms a group, dietitians form a group, security personnel form a group, and on and on. You can begin to see what a complicated social system a hospital, or any institution, actually is. And each of these groups has to relate in some way with the other groups if it is going to get its job done. We know that isn't easy. Frictions do arise.

How does one group communicate with another group? Clearly each person in each group cannot talk with each person in every other group. That would amount to chaos. So each group must have its own spokesman. As a spokesman he becomes a leader. A leader, of course, must bear authority and exercise authority. The question then becomes, how does a group choose its spokesman and leader? How does it determine the authority it will give the leader, and how much?

This is where the Tavistock approach comes in. It is interested in all these group processes. The Tavistock goal is to make participants at its conferences increasingly aware of how a group functions and why. Conference themes for the past few years have centered on leadership and the uses of authority.

The Tavistock-Washington School of Psychiatry method requires participants to attend a one- or two-week conference. Here each participant becomes a member of a small group. The task of each group is to study its own behavior. All small groups meet together to form one large group, the large group then providing an opportunity for all to observe how a large group operates. The small groups also examine and learn from intergroup events, the relationships between and among groups as they occur. Finally, toward the end of each conference application groups are formed of up to ten people engaged in the same type of work in their regular lives. These groups prepare participants to apply what they have learned at the conferences to problems back home.

Note that these Group Relations Conferences are strictly educational, not therapeutic, in intent. The emphasis is on learning and work rather than therapeutic relief or personal growth.

Address: The A. K. Rice Institute of
            The Washington School of Psychiatry
            1610 New Hampshire Avenue, N.W.
            Washington, D.C. 20009

XII

Parting Thoughts

Humor

Is there a place for humor in groups? Indeed there is! If a sense of humor is a sign of good health in a person, it is equally a sign of good health in a group.

If you find yourself in a group where nobody ever laughs, take care. Something's wrong. Ask yourself what's happening. There's no need for the group to be grim all the time. If it is, you have a sick group.

Consistent absence of humor and laughter in a group is apt to be found when interaction among the members of the group is stifled. On the other hand, when group members feel free to interact with each other the occasion for humor will arise naturally, spontaneously. I remember an instance when a man was telling of his anger toward his wife, how she'd make him so mad he would start breaking dishes —over her head! Someone asked, "How did she feel about that?" He replied, "She frowned on it." Nobody could keep a straight face at that one. And another time, the woman who remarked, "I can't talk to my husband when he's mad, so I talk to my dog." Then, with a sigh, she added, "If that dog could only talk!" Not meant to be funny but it was and the group broke up in laughter.

An inexperienced leader will frequently restrict interaction because of his mistaken notion of what group therapy is. He may be laboring under the assumption that the whole burden of making the group work rests on his shoulders. He therefore conducts the group as though he were holding one-way interviews with each patient, going around the group asking question after question after question of one person after another. The group members begin to feel they're in a kind of verbal straitjacket they can't break out of. Resistances develop and show up in a number of ways. The leader begins to get a little desperate, especially since he doesn't grasp what's happening. At this point thoughts of giving up the group may pop into his mind.

Humor is life saving. Laughter brings relief. Tensions ease. Laughter also holds people together. Though it may sound corny to say so, the group that laughs together is more likely to stay together.

A Touch of Theory

What is there about therapy groups that makes them work? Is it all just a matter of technique and the skill of the therapist? Though the therapist's orientation and what (s) he does is important, of course, I think that is only part of the answer.

The rest of the answer lies in the very nature of a group of human beings who come together for their common good. I have seen many groups and they included people with all sorts of symptoms, worries, anxieties, and problems, just about everything except outright psychoses. Provided the therapists allowed them the freedom to be themselves, these groups all moved toward health and well-being, and the patients improved. This kind of group provides the necessary favorable climate for emotional growth.

In this psychological climate the healthy, positive elements within the group seem to merge and cumulate, whereas the unhealthy, negative elements seem to remain separate and are non-cumulative. Put another way, the healthy aspects are centripetal, moving toward the center and becoming mutually reinforcing, while the diseased, pathological aspects are centrifugal, moving away from the center, and are therefore largely incapable of reinforcing each other. Quite simply, the healthy elements overcome the unhealthy ones.

This latent health-giving power which lies within human beings is awesome indeed. It will make an optimist out of you once you observe it, and leave you with the feeling there is yet hope for mankind.

And Finally, the Human in Humanity

We've taken a look at group psychotherapy and the small group field. Just opened the door to glance in, really. We've noted how the two have grown since the days of World War II to stand so big on the social scene today. But we haven't asked how come? How do we account for the phenomenal growth of "groups"?

Granted that people need treatment (group therapy) and people need education (small group field), are these two needs alone sufficient in themselves to account for the growth we've seen? I think not.

Many writers have commented recently on how mechanical our society has become, how impersonal it is in so many ways. And we seem to be headed toward more of the same. Machines appear to be taking over. We're losing our names and becoming numbers. "Don't give me your name. Give me your number." We hear this more and more. People used to worry that we would lose out to automation. But currently automation seems to have given way to the computer. In any case, people feel increasingly dehumanized by society, however much we may admire that same society as an advanced civilization. How can we fight this dehumanizing process, how can we stop it? How can we hold on to the precious feeling of being human?

I believe people are turning to "groups" as the answer. We're moving to groups in protest and reaction to the mechanical world in which we must live. A person's identity means everything to him or her. The identity that people are in danger of losing to numbers they are able to reestablish in groups. For in these groups nobody is a number. People discover other people, and people become persons. This amounts to an upsurge in humanism. People are looking to each other.

Many years ago L. C. Marsh, one of the pioneers in the field of group therapy, had a credo: "By the crowd they have been broken; by the crowd they shall be healed." The deep desire to remain and to be fully human gives new meaning to the words, ". . . by the crowd they shall be healed."

Figures show that "groups" are gaining steadily in numbers while church attendance continues to drop off dramatically. Perhaps people are finding more security in humanism than in superhumanism. God knows.

XIII

Where to Go for More

You can get useful leads to further reading from books and articles in professional journals. At the end of an article and at the end of a chapter in a book, sometimes at the end of the book, you will find lists of references to other articles and books on related topics. Following this path into the literature has the major advantage that when the articles and books are recent publications the references they cite will be recent, too, keeping you up-to-date with the latest contributions in the field.

Below is a list of important articles and books. It is purposely short and highly selective, with brief comments you may find helpful.

The publications are arranged by category. You'll discover that one or another topic or subject you expect to find may seem to be missing. Don't despair. You will probably find it in one of the general books as the subject of an article in the collected papers. For example, you won't see bioenergetics listed as a separate category but you will find Alexander Lowen's paper on Bio-energetic Group Therapy in Ruitenbeek's *Group Therapy Today*. Check it out.

GENERAL

BACH, G. A. *Intensive group psychotherapy*. New York: Ronald Press, 1954.

> A classic by a modern pioneer. Part I and Part II is

solid basic group therapy; Part III, which deals with
theory, may be safely omitted.

BERGER, M. Nonverbal communications in group psychotherapy. *International Journal of Group Psychotherapy.*
1958, 8, 161-178.

> A lot goes on in groups without a word being spoken.
> This paper will alert you to unspoken communica-
> tions and start you on the way to catching them.

LIEBERMAN, M., YALOM, I., & MILES, M. *Encounter
groups: first facts.* New York: Basic Books, 1973.

> The results of research. "Encounter" is loose usage
> here because therapy groups are included among the
> 17 different types of groups reported on.

PARLOFF, M. B. Group therapy and the small group field:
an encounter. *International Journal of Group Psychotherapy,* 1970, 20, 267-304.

> Makes a distinction between group therapy and the
> small group field, and takes a critical look at the
> present-day scene.

POWDERMAKER, F. & FRANK, J. *Group Psychotherapy.*
Cambridge, Massachusetts: Harvard University Press,
1953.

> A classic in the field, the result of research with pa-
> tient groups in hospitals and clinics of the Veterans
> Administration just after World War II. Skip the
> statistical stuff. What remains is rich clinical ma-
> terial. For example, the authors found that in almost
> every therapy group certain easily identifiable per-
> sonality types emerge—such as the doctor's assistant,
> the help-rejecting complainer, the self-righteous
> moralist, the injustice collector. You'll find them in
> your groups, too.

ROSENBAUM, M. & BERGER, M. M. (Eds.) *Group psychotherapy and group function.* New York: Basic Books,
1963.

A collection of basic readings, this book will save you hours of library time—even if you could locate all the selections, some of which are hard to find.

RUITENBEEK, H. M. (Ed.) *Group therapy today.* New York: Atherton Press, 1969.

A collection of papers by different authors of proven competence. Articles on group therapy from the point of view of the more traditional schools of Adler, Horney, and Harry Stack Sullivan. Several articles on problems in traditional group therapy and an equal number of papers on recent trends.

SAGER, C. J. & KAPLAN, H. S. (Eds.) *Progress in group and family therapy.* New York: Brunner/Mazel, 1972.

A collection of papers by leaders in these areas. Worth having, although lack of an index severely limits its usefulness as a reference source.

YALOM, I. D. *The theory and practice of group psychotherapy.* New York: Basic Books, 1970.

Consider it an advanced textbook. Up-to-date, it covers most angles, citing numerous references. A scholarly work.

COUPLES

BACH, G. R. & WYDEN, P. *The intimate enemy.* New York: W. M. Morrow, 1969.

Details the constructive use of aggression, the Fair Fight Technique for married couples.

GESTALT

FAGAN, J. & SHEPHERD, I. (Eds.) *Gestalt therapy now.* Palo Alto; Science & Behavior Books, 1970.

Clarifies many of the concepts of Gestalt therapy. A must book if you are professionally interested in Gestalt.

POLSTER, E. & POLSTER, M. *Gestalt therapy integrated: contours of theory and practice.* New York: Brunner/ Mazel, 1973.

SCHUTZ, W. *Joy: expanding human awareness.* New York: Grove Press, 1967.

> Exercises to tie in with the Gestalt awareness continuum. Useful in any group.

PSYCHOANALYSIS IN GROUPS

FOULKES, S. H. & ANTHONY, E. J. *Group psychotherapy: the psychoanalytic approach.* Baltimore: Penguin Books, 1965.

> The authors write in the literate English tradition of psychoanalysis.

SYNANON

CASRIEL, D. *So fair a house.* Englewood Cliffs, New Jersey: Prentice-Hall, 1963.

> Another account of Synanon.

MASLOW, A. Synanon and eupsychia. In Ruitenbeek, H. M. (Ed.), *Group therapy today.* New York: Atherton, 1969.

> Maslow is one of the foremost humanists of our time. Eupsychia = more fully human.

MASLOW, A. *Eupsychian management.* Homewood, Illinois: Dow-Jones-Erwin, 1965.

> Title is self-explanatory.

T-GROUPS AND LABORATORY TRAINING

BRADFORD, L. P., GIBB, J. R., & BENNE, K. D. (Eds.) *T-group theory and laboratory method.* New York: Wiley, 1964.

A book of readings that has become a standard reference.

LUBIN, B. & EDDY, W. B. The laboratory training model: rationale, method, and some thoughts for the future. *International Journal of Group Psychotherapy*, 1970, 20, 305-339.

A good brief overview.

SCHEIN, E. H. & BENNIS, W. G. *Personal and organizational change through group method: the laboratory approach*. New York: John Wiley and Sons, 1965.

A respected textbook.

Index

Ackerman, Nathan W., 151
Adler, Alfred, 14
Adult education, 19
Aha! experience, 69
Alcoholism, 101, 107, 163
Alexander, Franz, 83, 83 n
Allen, Frederick H., 83 n
Ambisexual. *See* Homosexuality, bisexual
American Academy of Psychotherapists (AAP), 153-154
American Group Psychotherapy Association (AGPA), 14, 132, 154-155
American Society of Group Psychotherapy and Psychodrama (ASGPP), 155-156
Anxieties, 12, 21, 27-28, 34, 66, 139
Association for Humanistic Psychology, 158-159
Attitudes, 29
    patient, 21, 53, 69, 143
    therapist, 83-84
Authority figure, 15, 21, 39, 165
Awareness, levels of, 28
Awareness continuum, 139

Bach, George R., 148
Basic Skills Training Group (BST), 19, 161
Beginning Stage. *See* Psychotherapy groups, continuous (open-ended), beginning stage of

Behavior, 10-11, 12, 52-53, 54, 55-56, 79, 165
    disorders of, 101-102
    points of view of, 55-56
    understanding of, 10
Behavior Modification, 54-55
Benne, Kenneth D., 17
Berne, Eric, 54, 133-135, 159
Bibliography, 171-175
    couples, 173
    general, 171-173
    Gestalt, 173-174
    Psychoanalysis in groups, 174
    Synanon, 174
    T-groups and laboratory training, 174-175
Bisexual. *See* Homosexuality, bisexual
Body language, 12, 76
Bradford, Leland P., 17

Catharsis, 141
Centre for Applied Social Research of the Tavistock Institute of London, 164-166
Change agents, 7-8, 19, 63, 98, 161, *See also* Leaders
Choice points, 50, 59-63
Client-centered therapy, xvi, 62, 143-144, 147. *See also* Rogers, Dr. Carl R.
Closed group. *See* Psychotherapy groups, closed